THE OTHER FRANCIS

THE OTHER FRANCIS

EVERYTHING THEY DID NOT TELL YOU ABOUT THE POPE

DEBORAH CASTELLANO LUBOV

PREFACE BY CARDINAL PIETRO PAROLIN

GRACEWING

First published in 2018 by
Gracewing
2 Southern Avenue
Leominster
Herefordshire HR6 0QF
United Kingdom
www.gracewing.co.uk

ISBN 978 085244 934 9

Typeset by Gracewing

Cover design by Bernardita Peña Hurtado

I dedicate this book to my parents, Judy and Phil
and to my husband, Paolo Fucili

CONTENTS

ACKNOWLEDGEMENTS

I WOULD LIKE TO thank from the bottom of my heart two collaborators, who are also dear friends, Dr Michael Hesemann and Giuseppe Sabella.

Dr Michael Hesemann, the famous German author and historian, known for having co-authored *My Brother the Pope* with Georg Ratzinger among many others, has granted me the great honour of including in this work his exclusive interviews done in Buenos Aires with Maria Elena Bergoglio, Pope Francis's sister, and Chief Rabbi of Buenos Aires Abraham Skorka. These conversations of yours are truly priceless and add such heart to the book's collection of interviews.

Turning to Giuseppe, Director of Think-In based in Milan, research fellow at the Donald Lynch Foundation in the US, and author known for his economic expertise, your support from the beginning and throughout the process really helped me bring from what was an idea into a finished product, especially with its original Italian publication of *L'Altro Francesco*, with the prestigious Cantagalli of Siena. Your insights into human dignity and economic matters helped me explore profoundly various aspects of this pontificate.

Both of your support helped bring this work to fruition. *Danke* and *Grazie!*

PREFACE

T HE EASE WITH which Pope Francis appeared to the world at the start of his papacy is something relatively new, and is shaping the Church from within. The friendship that the Pope shows for the Christian people—which is ultimately a desire to walk together—is the same friendship that he shows to those who have chosen to follow Christ in the priesthood and who need daily to be renewed by returning to the source of their mission.

In the following interviews it will be no surprise to hear people, including some who hold high office in the Church, share the amazing effect of their personal encounters with Francis. They feel themselves welcomed by a look, by Francis's look, so full of affection and mercy, sentiments that give rise to our sense of human dignity.

Francis is carrying out this great service: at a time when technology and money seem to reign supreme, he shows the men and women of today, affected by a crisis which is often more spiritual than economic, the only way to rediscover the true value of being human. That way is Jesus, as he himself tells us in the Gospel of John: 'I am the way, and the truth, and the life' (Jn 14:6).

With humility, but also with tireless perseverance, the Pope daily reminds us priests of the demands of the Gospel, whether by his words or actions, or by his concern for the poor and the needy. Man does not live on bread alone, yet he needs bread to survive. And today, in the midst of a great crisis, there are many who lack that bread.

Pope Francis's emphasis on poverty has also characterized his entire ministry as Pastor of the Church and his witness to Christ. To me what best captures this Pontificate is the moment in Florence, at the San Francesco Poverino soup kitchen, when the Pope poured water into the plastic cup of an elderly woman, holding a plastic jug himself.

The concern of Francis for the poor, however, must not be confused with sentimental ideas about poverty or charitable assistance. In attending to the least of our brothers and sisters, we experience the reality of charity, and thus of Christ. So it is in Matthew's Gospel: 'As you did it to one of the least of these my brethren, you did it to me' (Mt 25:40). In John's Gospel this is clearer still when Jesus warns, 'The poor you always have with you, but you do not always have me' (Jn 12:8).

For this reason, Pope Francis continually invites us to understand the poor and to be attentive to them as people, not just to their material necessities but also to the needs of their hearts. For our hearts, like theirs, are in need of Christ.

The evident love of Francis for the Son of God has made a great impression even on those who do not believe. Many non-believers have expressed their wonder and curiosity about this Pope and, in some way, about the word of God. This is a sign that today, as ever, the Holy Spirit is alive and at work in the Church.

Pietro Cardinal Parolin
Vatican Secretary of State

INTRODUCTION

WHAT AM I, a former Certified Public Accountant from New York City doing every day in the Vatican, on *Via Della Conciliazione*, rather than being among the skyscrapers of Manhattan? When God has a plan for you, not even one's own plans can deviate its course.

Growing up in close proximity of New York City led me to dream and have aspirations of becoming a corporate attorney working on Wall Street. I was very close to achieving that dream, when I believe I was called to another.

I did achieve the dream of working on Wall Street, and that is where I experienced the outcome of the Conclave of 2013. I was on my lunch break in front of the New York Stock Exchange in the Financial District of New York City. The normal rhythm of lunchtime on Wall Street involves business people weaving in and out around tourists slowing down to marvel at the sights, and stockbrokers smoking outside and talking. That particular day I was pacing and anxiously watching the Pope App as it transmitted the news of white smoke being seen from the Sistine Chapel chimney. I heard the announcement of 'Habemus Papam'... followed by the name, Bergoglio. I was very excited, as it felt very personal to me. During college, I had an internship at the Vatican; therefore, I could visualize the day's events as they unfolded. When I returned to my office on Wall Street, I was greeted by the excitement among the security guards of Puerto Rican heritage. They were thrilled that this Pope spoke their native language! This was just a microscopic look into the future excitement our new Holy Father would inspire.

I always desired to return to Rome, more specifically the Vatican. During my experience at the Pontifical Council of Social Communications I realized this is where I was meant to be. I changed my plans: instead of attending law school I was recruited by a 'Big Four' accounting firm (Pricewaterhouse Coopers) and became a Certified Public Accountant. My career was going very well, but it was not my true calling and in my heart and soul I knew I must return to Rome. I knew my true vocation was to serve the Church in the area of communications. I took a leap of faith and moved to Rome. God led me to this decision and in my heart, I knew He had chosen this vocation for me.

This is how I found myself in Rome, as a Vatican correspondent, where Saint Peter built the Catholic Church, the Church of Christ, under the pontificate of the 265th Successor of Peter, Pope Francis. The election of Cardinal Jorge Mario Bergoglio as Pope, who came from the 'ends of the earth' had generated interest by Catholic and non-Catholic international media and throughout the world.

The pontificate of Pope Benedict XVI finished with his resounding and unexpected resignation. At the time I was saddened as I had a deep love and admiration for him, but this was God's plan. Now there seems to be a new wind breezing through, offering daily surprises raising a renewed interest in the Church.

I, as a journalist, had the desire to speak with as many 'insiders,' if you will, to orient myself in that environment.

I was seeking 'unfiltered' sources, without interpretations. It was not acceptable for me to report on that which had already been said by others, items from 'experts' that 'believe' to know, or even worse, those that manipulate the news.

I was seeking the voices of those who truly know Francis up close, be it from the position they hold or through a personal relationship. It was important to have voices that offer an original look at the Pope from a broader view, reflecting the universality of the Church.

This book is the fruit of that research performed in the normal responsibilities of my career. Starting from contacts and friendships that had come to be over time, I began to inquire from these various 'insiders', their availability to have relaxed, in-depth conversations in which they would tell me about 'their Francis.'

Many influential and authoritative individuals granted their availability to depict an unedited portrait, full of shades and colours until then unknown. The idea, shared with my publisher, who I thank, transformed this idea into reality and the book little by little came to life and now has been brought to life in Italian, Spanish, Lithuanian versions and potentially others.

To my surprise, the roster of the interviewees was enriched by illustrious names: the Vatican Secretary of State, Cardinal Pietro Parolin, who wrote the preface and to whom I express my heartfelt gratitude; the Cardinals Gerhard Ludwig Muller, Peter Kodwo Appiah Turkson, Kurt Koch, and George Pell; the Prefect of the Papal Household, Archbishop Georg Ganswein. I thought also of involving principal leaders of the Church from five continents, those who live far away geographically speaking from the See of Peter, united however to it through the Ecclesial Communion which surpasses every burden: the Latin Patriarch Emeritus of Jerusalem, His Beatitude Fouad Twal; Cardinal Charles Maung Bo, Archbishop of Yangon in Myanmar; Archbishop Joseph Edward Kurtz, Archbishop of Louisville and President Emeritus of the United States Conference of Catholic Bishops; Cardinal Timothy Dolan, Archbishop of New York; Cardinal Wilfrid Fox Napier, Archbishop of Durban in South Africa.

Two truly exclusive interviews give charm and depth to the volume, namely the sister of the Pope, Maria Elena Bergoglio and that of the lead rabbi of Buenos Aires Abraham Skorka. They were both conducted by Dr Michael Hesemann, the famous German author and historian who honours me with his friendship, and who co-authored the famous book *My Brother the Pope with Georg Ratzinger*.

To complete the painting are Father Federico Lombardi, former director of the Holy See Press Office, who always welcomed me cordially, offering always his availability, and also a dear and longtime friend of Cardinal Bergoglio of Buenos Aires, Adrian Pallarols, a young master silversmith, following an illustrious family tradition in the Argentinean capital. 'Son, Brother, Friend' exclaimed Pope Francis with a huge grin during our first encounter when I told the Holy Father that Adrian was our friend in common.

Recalling my chance encounter with Adrian, one morning in NYC I was uncertain whether to stop as I usually did in St Patrick's Cathedral to pray before starting work. I used to regularly remind the Lord of my desire to return one day to Rome permanently. 'Today I am running late' I thought to myself. Arriving in front of the cathedral and deciding to enter, I immediately noticed a photo of Pope Benedict XVI and Cardinal Bergoglio who was giving the Pontiff a chalice created by Pallarols. It was displayed on a poster announcing an encounter with Pallarols happening that same evening. There was born my great friendship with the silversmith of the Pope. That being said, when Adrian arrives in Italy the second phone call often is for me. I let you wonder to whom he makes the first call.

Turning now to the Pope Emeritus, of whom I had the blessing to encounter recently, I always keep his photo in a notebook under my computer. It was the April page in one of the tiny calendars sold in the souvenir shops near the Vatican. It gave me immense comfort to see his image during my hectic work day. I remember the morning, while on the bus towards Manhattan, I heard the strange words announced in Latin, 'Conscientia mea iterum atque iterum coram Deo explorata ... Declaro me ministerio Episcopi Romae ... Renuntiare ...' Pope Benedict has resigned. I remember it with absolute clarity. Thirty days later I would hear the proclamation of our new Pope while I was in front of the New York Stock Exchange. At these profound moments, I knew God was speaking to me.

I conclude with a sincere wish that this book could give a small contribution for better understanding the thought, the spirituality, and humanity of Francis, redesigning the aspects, at times deformed or altered in unrecognizable and unfortunately manipulated ways.

Every supreme pontiff in the history of the Church has his role and function in the painting of a project that remains often misunderstood and unfathomable. The Designer works with a steady and sure hand knowing with certainty that which man needs at all times to live an existence full of meaning and of dignity. The people of God have this certainty knowing that everything happens according to God's plan and that each person is loved in an immeasurable and unconditional way with a full and infinite mercy. The helm of the ship of Peter is as always in good hands.

I hope to offer a reader witness of those who have the privilege of a relationship with the Holy Father, of those who love him and are loved by him, and who know him well, even in the less known personal aspects.

It is he, Pope Francis, who shows us how wonderful and acceptable it is to 'follow the beat of your own drum' even at times if it often means not conforming to those around you. After all, many saints were great 'non-conformists', or at least people who did not keep their dreams in a drawer. I, too, not being a saint, had a dream and I followed it. This book is part of that dream. I hope it can be a help in deepening and understanding better the man who shows us to be ourselves, knowing God is at our side and to not be afraid to dream.

1 Maria Elena Bergoglio

Sister of Jorge Mario Bergoglio, Pope Francis

'I pray that nothing and nobody extinguishes the flame of the Holy Spirit in his heart.'

Maria Elena Bergoglio on her brother, Pope Francis

Michael Hesemann[1]

T HE SUBURB ITUZAINGO where Maria Elena Bergoglio, the 64-year-old sister of the Pope lives together with her son Jorge in a simple but nice house, is about an hour from Barrio San Nicolas, the city centre of Buenos Aires. It is a comfortable not quite middle-class suburb with orderly little houses behind small front yards. In front of the Bergoglio house waits a police car, the house curtains are drawn shut, and the inhabitants are more secluded after the turmoil of the past six weeks. Only after trying for days, my Argentinian colleague Molly Maria Hamilton-Baillie managed to convince Maria Elena to meet for a conversation. Now she accompanies me as an interpreter.

I ring the door bell, dogs start barking, and the curtain is pushed to the side. Immediately a curious black snout starts to inspect me. As I will find out later this snout belongs to the passionate, playful, clumsy, and incredible endearing Labrador she-dog Iris, which is only held back by Jorge, the nephew of the Pope, who is trying to prevent her from kicking over people and furniture alike. Iris is locked into a room, while Maria Elena Bergoglio welcomes us into her house.

The greeting is cordial and she opens up immediately while I look into her fascinating warm brown eyes which remind me time and time again of the mystical glance of the Pope. Maybe a trace of melancholy shines through, but there is definitely profundity and warmth in them. Her son Jorge is shyer and does not want to speak. He is a tall friendly young man with long hair in a comfortable track suit, who works as an architect in the school of Buckminster Fuller's multifunctional structure made from geodesic domes. At the end of the interview he brings a glass of Mate-tea: one glass only, of course, since Mate is drank in a shared way. The pleasure of the slightly bitter Argentinian national drink is a ritual of peace. The mug with the herbs onto which hot water is poured goes around and one after the other drinks from the straw. We already feel accepted into the family. I am even allowed to play with Iris.

Mrs Bergoglio...

Please call me Maria Elena!

With pleasure, Maria Elena. In an interview with my American colleague, John L. Allen of the National Catholic Reporter, you explained that you would like to congratulate Georg Ratzinger for his brother. If you had the possibility now, what would you tell him?

First and foremost, I would like to thank him from the depth of my heart for his brother. Benedict XVI was a great and extraordinary Pope, even if many people could not recognise it. He had a difficult position as the successor of St John Paul II, who was very charismatic and swept up the hearts of the faithful with his personality. We were, and I am including myself, unfair towards him because he was an introverted and shy intellectual. We must remember that Cardinal Ratzinger was responsible for the most important reflections and documents of Pope John Paul II's pontificate. I needed some time to discover him for myself, his great inner wealth. As Pope he began to disclose the problems and the scandals of the Church, which is a difficult task, but he did it without hesitation. He had the right humility, courage, and honesty when he gave up his position of Pope, a position of power. Who today would give something like that up? That is why I honour him. Luckily more and more Christians recognise that he was a great Pope and that he is an extraordinary man who showed courage in every way.

I promise you that I will pass on your words to Msgr Georg Ratzinger. Let us now focus on your brother. When he travelled to the Conclave did you have an idea that he would become Pope? Did he take that into consideration?

It was never a topic of discussion. He never thought that he would become Pope and I could not wait for him to come back. Before his return he called me and told me, 'Okay, girl, I am leaving now. Please pray for me and pray for the Conclave. We will see each other once I am back.' I was fully calm at heart, since I never expected that with the outcome he would never return. Personally, I would have wished for Cardinal Scherer as the new Pope, while my son Jorge would have preferred to have one of the Franciscan Cardinals, such as Carlos Amigo Vallejo, Cláudio Hummes, Wilfrid Fox Napier, or Sean Patrick O'Malley.

How did you experience the Habemus Papam! 'We have a Pope?'

I was here in my house with my son. We had obviously turned on the TV and we saw the white smoke. We went on with our daily chores and between them commented on what the reporters talked about in the moment. I was joking a little when they talked about the 'room of tears' but it never crossed my mind that the chosen one really would cry if he thought about the large square full of people who waited for him. How could you not cry? [In this moment tears came into the eyes of Maria Elena]

The only thing I heard of the Habemus Papam, 'We have a Pope' was Georgius Marius, Jorge Mario. I did not even hear the last name, I was so overwhelmed, indeed shocked. More and more people came to my house, happy people; and the telephone rang the whole day. Since that day, I cannot really comprehend what happened in that moment. The next day at 6 o'clock in the morning the TV cameras were all in front of my house. It way crazy but at the same time wonderful! The reporters were very nice to me as I opened the door and came out to them. I am very thankful for these reporters for their respectful behaviour and their courtesy.

Did you watch as he was presented to the faithful on the loggia? What was your impression? What was different in him?

Of course, I saw him stepping on the balcony. He remained the same. He was the same Jorge whom I have always known. I had only a little time to think about it after they said his name, since our house became a beehive. Everyone called or rang the door; it was truly pure chaos. When I finally had the chance to think about it and to re-visit the images, I had the impression that he was really happy in that moment. It seemed like the Holy Spirit was with him in that moment. I also think that he is very joyful still. He was very close to the people of Argentina, but now he seems to be even closer to them. He has now more occasions to express his feelings and I think that the Holy Spirit is helping him. It fills me with joy to see how my brother has grown into that role.

The office is also a large burden.

Yes, it is. I think that he is happy about the responsibility which was given to him, even knowing that it is large and burdensome.

When did you speak to him for the first time after his election?

He called me right after; it was a very emotional talk. It is difficult to explain what I felt in that moment.

What did he say?

We spoke as is common among siblings, 'How are you?' I repeated the question and he only responded, 'How could I not have called you now?' I answered, 'I would like to hug you now.' He said, 'Believe me you are doing it just now!'

Did he seem overwhelmed?

He seemed like always. He seemed neither nervous nor agitated. Francis is still my brother Jorge!

How close is your contact with him since then?

He has called me many times since then. We always speak to one another like brother and sister. Very normal phone calls, just how they used to be. He asked, for example, what I was cooking. He has lots to do, of course. I would like to have more time with my brother, but that is now impossible. He calls me as often as possible. It is always him who calls me. I do not know how I could reach him. I do not even want to know, since I do not want to bother him.

Does he speak about his office as Pope at all and his plans for the Church?

No, we only speak about family topics, never about his work or his plans.

Did he tell you what Pope Benedict XVI told him as the Cardinals departed for the Conclave?

Yes, he did tell me. He was always very loyal. He flew to Rome on 26 February in order to participate in the farewell of the Pope. As the cardinals stepped in front of the Pope one by one, Benedict told Jorge, 'You owe me obedience. If you get elected, then you have to accept.'

Do you ever feel as though you have lost your brother, since he is completely taken up by his office now?

To be honest, I feel more like having received millions of new brothers and sisters. I only have to figure out how to share my brother with all these new family members! We did not see him much when he was Archbishop of Buenos Aires. Believe me, he did not even have time to visit me here in Ituzaingo. We spoke often on the phone, way too often and way too long.

When he calls you today, how do you address him; as 'Jorge' or as 'Holy Father'?

Of course, as 'Jorge'! As long as I know that it is my brother who is calling, I call him 'Jorge'! Maybe I will get used one day to calling him 'Francis'. At this point, he is simply Jorge for me!

Did you come to his taking of office in Rome? Do you plan on visiting him?

I am not sure, maybe in the summer. Perhaps I am still waiting for him to come to Argentina. I think that would make me a little bit scared.

Why?

Well, I think that every journalist believes that he would visit us in our house and then we would have a whole camp of them outside our house trying to participate. He would certainly not come here. If he comes to Argentina, he would come for a pastoral visit, not to go on vacation or to see his family. Of course, I would follow him and stay wherever he was. Even if he would only grant me two minutes, I would be happy. All that I want are two minutes in order to embrace him. I do not expect more from him.

Many things are inconsistent in the books written about your family. Sometimes it says that your father was a simple railway constructor, then that he was an accountant with the railway. Sometimes it says that your family fled to Argentina because of poverty, sometimes because of the fascists. What is the truth?

What on earth are the people imagining! [laughs] Our father never worked for the railway, but he was an accountant. Our family left Italy because of Mussolini.

Our grandmother was simply divine; she was a true dear heart! After Mass or the rosary, she would climb onto the pulpit and begin to preach against Mussolini, even though the Carabinieri sat in church with their machine pistols! [laughs] She was very courageous and very brave. At a certain point our grandparents simply had to leave Italy or Mussolini would have incarcerated them.

They lived in Turin. My father worked as an accountant at a bank in Turin, and our grandparents owned the finest café in town. During the day, they worked at the café, at night they turned it into an elegant bar. The tablecloths were exchanged and the tables and chairs were moved around, then drinks were served. They were well off even though they had to work hard for it.

It is said that your grandmother sewed cash money into her fur coat when she left for Buenos Aires in January, in the summer!

Yes, that is true. That is where she hid the money. In Argentina they lived at first in Entre Rios, Paraná, where my grandfather's brothers had a paving-stone factory which was very successful. The house in which they lived was known in the whole city as 'Bergoglio Palace', since it was so luxurious. It had four stories, a cast iron dome in the art nouveau style, and it was the only privately-owned house that had its own elevator. The world economic crisis came and the company went bankrupt. The family remained in Entre Rios until all their debts were paid, but then they were dispersed throughout the whole country. My great uncle Eugenio left for Córdoba, my granduncle Albino to Azul, our grandparents and our father left for Buenos Aires where they opened a grocery store. My father would have loved to work as an accountant again, but his diplomas were not recognized in Argentina. He would have practically needed to repeat his whole education. He did not want that. Therefore, he decided to work in the grocery store of our grandparents; to do the accounting, as well as, to deliver goods to clients on his bike. On the other side of the street there was a hosiery factory, and they finally employed him. He was an accountant there, even if he could never finish the books there.

Tell us about your mother?

My mother was from Argentina, daughter of an Italian and an Argentinian with roots in Genoa. Our parents met at church after Sunday Mass in the Basilica San Carlos Borromeo y Maria Auxilidora.

Who are venerated as the great saint and the patroness of Turin, their home town.

Yes, exactly. There they got married and we were all baptized, including Jorge Mario.

Can you describe her character?

Our mother had a strong, tough character and she really needed one too in order to raise five children. Our father too took part in our education, but he also had to work. Our mother was in charge of the household. She showed us her love through the things that she did for us. She was uncompromising. She did so much for us and was so joyful doing so.

She was a great lover of music, it is said.

Oh yes, she loved the opera. 'Madame Butterfly' was her favourite opera, but she also loved other composers of the classic period. Classical music was part of our life. Our parents went oftentimes with our older brothers to the Teatro Colón, the opera house of Buenos Aires.

Were your parents very strict or was there a rather relaxed atmosphere in your family?

Neither really. It was typical for mother and father to teach by example. They did not give long family dialogues or great speeches. They told us very simple things, so that we immediately understood what they wanted to tell us. Their words were always conveyed with concrete examples. I always experienced my parents as joyful and open. They were friends with other families and led a very open household. Additionally, they were active in our church community, very active, in fact.

Our house always belonged to us children. We did not have to leave in order to play or to have fun. On the weekends we often met with our relatives. Our father was a true family man. He did not spoil us, quite the opposite. We did not have all the material goods that we desired, but nothing was lacking either. Most of all, our father was a very pious man. He prayed the rosary with us every day. He always said to our mother: one day when you die, I will enter a monastery and become a monk.

Your brother often speaks about your grandmother whom he must have loved significantly.

Oh yes, that he did. She might have had the greatest influence on Jorge Mario's religious education. She also played an important role in his vocation, his beloved nonna, 'grandmother'. She was a courageous and deeply pious woman. I have many beautiful memories of her.

What are your earliest memories of him, of Jorge?

Jorge Mario is my brother and my best friend. He is twelve years older than me, so he was basically an adult by the time I can first remember him. He was always joyful and supported me, as it is right for an older brother to do. We always remained in contact; we wrote letters and called each other. We had a kind of a long-distance relationship. He was always present in my life, even in the distance. He will remain to be even now.

What were his hobbies as a boy?

He liked to read and he loved soccer, that was his passion. He always played on the small field, Herminia Brumana, at the corner of our house in the Membrillar Road. He loved classical music, as did my whole family; but he also was a very normal boy who had many friends. In his youth he listened to the typical music of the time, went to parties with his friends, and liked to dance.

Amalia Damote tells the story that Jorge fell in love with her and asked for her hand in marriage, but was rejected by her dad, is that true?

Please, stop it! Honestly, I have nothing against this person, but what stories she tells! Back then twelve-year-old girls played with dolls and boys with marbles. Children did not fall in love with each other; that simply did not happen. Nothing of what that woman tells is true!

He did have a girlfriend later, of whom he speaks in his interview book *El Jesuita*: 'She belonged to a group of friends with whom we went dancing.'

Well, he never spoke at home about it. He never said who this girl was.

How did you learn about his vocation?

After his schooling he told mother that he wanted to become a doctor. Mother was very happy, of course and said, 'Then I will make a room for you on the first floor, so that you can study in peace.' One day as she cleaned the room, she found many books which dealt with philosophy, theology, and Latin. She confronted him about it, 'Jorge, why did you lie to me?' 'Mother I did not lie to you', he responded calmly, 'I want to be a doctor of souls.'

Our father was overjoyed about this decision. He wanted a house full of nuns and priests. Mother had a more difficult time accepting this and tried at first to make him change his mind. Her problem was not so much the vocation in itself, but the idea that he would leave the house and the family for good. She did not want him to go. He wanted to join the Jesuits at all costs and dreamt of being a missionary in Asia.

What did that mean to you?

I was a small girl. I did not really have an opinion about it. I only knew that Jorge would not live with us then anymore, he would be far away. Since he wanted to become a priest, we had to pray for him a lot.

Then he got a strong lung infection.

He had already entered seminary. I recall that he was in a very precarious state, and we were very afraid of what would happen to him. He almost died. The doctors discovered three cysts in his right lung and had to remove the upper half. I remember that he recovered quickly. His dream of becoming a missionary was thwarted; the superiors would not let him do that because of his health situation.

Was he politically active then? It was the time of Peron.

Yes, he identified with Peronism, at least in its early period. The fundamentals of this movement agreed with the social doctrine of the Church. He was never left or right, for him only the message of the Gospel was important.

After the death of Peron and the overthrow of his wife Isabel, the military took over in Argentina. Back then your brother was already Provincial of the Jesuits at

the young age of 30. It is said that he struck a bargain with the Junta.

Do you believe that's possible? That would have meant that he had forgotten the example that our grandmother gave us with her life decisions. She fled from the fascists, and Jorge is supposed to have been in cahoots with a dictator? Never! It would have meant his betrayal of his beloved *nonna*, 'grandmother'!

Afterwards, he continued with his studies and went to Germany to pursue his doctorate. What did he say about Germany?

Not much, to be honest. He loved Germany, but he never spoke about the places he visited there.

When he was back in Argentina you formed your own family. How was he as an uncle for your children?

He joked a lot and always did shenanigans. He loved my son named Jorge the most, just like him. Once when Jorge Jr was a baby, Jorge dipped his sucker into whiskey and gave it back to him. My son was obviously very happy about that, as you can imagine. [laughs]

Did he visit you often back then?

No. Jorge Mario never really visited the houses of his siblings; he was never much with us, although he is a family person. He can be very funny. He is a true buddy and a lifelong companion.

Did you ever accompany him on one of his trips?

Yes, in 1998, when he received the Pallium as Archbishop of Buenos Aires, he took me to Italy. We visited Porta-comaro, the village our grandparents were from, before they went to Turin. The area is wonderful, and we wandered together through the hills. It was very moving to see the house in which my father was born, the garden in which he played as a child, and the basement in which our uncle once made wine. We were overwhelmed by so many emotions.

What impression did you have of Rome?

I was fascinated. I remember well the ruins of ancient Rome and my prayer at the tomb of St Peter. We drove one day to Assisi and that was a shock for me. The city had been destroyed shortly beforehand by an earthquake in September 1997 and despite that, I kept finding evidence of God's presence among the ruins. He was there! Assisi was destroyed, but the squares where St Francis had preached were intact or at least almost intact, I asked myself time and time again, what is the meaning of this? The Basilica of St Clara was heavily damaged, but I turned around and I saw the incorrupt completely intact body of this great saint, who laid there, as if she was only asleep. It moved me deeply and strengthened my faith. The images of the presence of God in Assisi after the earthquake didn't want to leave my head.

Was Assisi more impressive than Rome, for you?

To be honest, yes. If you ask me, I would prefer the Catholic Church in the model of Assisi. From my impressions of the presence of God in Assisi, I could not go into the Vatican after my time in Assisi, it was not important anymore to me. I marvelled at the artwork there, the rich cultural heritage; but I prefer the church of Assisi.

How will your brother change the Church of Rome?

Many things will change. We constantly see new things, something changing. He does not live in the Apostolic Palace. He explained to me that his dream is a Church for the poor. That is the essence of all that he tries to communicate. A Church that should get rid of her riches and privileges and whose shepherds 'take on the smell of the sheep', not remaining distant or high above the faithful avoiding contact with them, but who live with the people and serve them. That is also the reason why he refused to wear the red shoes which are a sign of kingship. The pope is not a king but a servant of God. He will need some time to give the Church a new face, because this can only happen in slow steps. He wants to change the Roman Curia as well. It is a reason why some cardinals react to his gestures and try to imitate him. This is the way in which he has always communicated, not only with words, but mostly by his own example.

In Europe he received euphoric acceptance!

I am very happy about the fact that he has been received positively in Europe. It is a revolution for Europe and the world. Whoever wants change must change himself first. That is only possible in daily life. We have to look at God's grace and trust. Behind everything that Jorge does as Pope Francis is Jesus himself. We should never leave Jesus out of our sight.

Will he be able to push through?

I have no doubt about that. He has a strong character, a very strong character. He believes very strongly in his convictions. Nobody will be able to change his mind. He is not made for compromises when dealing with something that he believes in. He will be a good Pope. He is made for that!

How much Jorge Mario Bergoglio will be present in Pope Francis? Will he be able to keep going?

Francis is still Jorge and he carries the Gospel in his heart. That will help him to be a good Pope. We have to pray for him.

When you pray for him, what do you ask for?

I pray to the Holy Spirit and in these prayers my brother Jorge, our Pope Francis, always figures first. I pray that the Holy Spirit gives him inner strength and consolation, and that nothing and nobody extinguish his inner flame of the Holy Spirit.

Thank you, Maria Elena!

2 Cardinal Charles Maung Bo, SDB

Archbishop of Yangon, Myanmar

Enhance and Encourage the Periphery

In Pope Francis's consistories, the surprises have been many. Some were even surprised when Francis decided to appoint the Archbishop of Yangon a cardinal. Were you as well?

POPE FRANCIS SURPRISED all of us beyond any expectations. Myanmar was known for its long struggle for democracy, its democratic icon Daw Aung San Sui Kyi was known to the world. When the news that a bishop from Myanmar had been appointed cardinal, the world wanted to know about this part of the Church.

While I am surprised about his choice, I was not shocked, since he has always insisted on 'perspectives from the margin.' What he preaches, he practices. When choosing to appoint new cardinals, the Pope remembered a tiny little Catholic population of Myanmar, just 700,000 people. This is his way of empowering the margins.

Another surprising gesture on the occasion of Francis's consistories, was to recommend to the new cardinals to have sober celebrations, without wasting money. How should we interpret this gesture?

Pope Francis has been insisting on 'power that comes from service', not pomp and glory. He has been trying through his life and mission to recast the Church as the Church of the poor and for the poor. Once the Church was a major player in power and glory, and triumphalism sometimes marked Her activities. This call to simplicity was not a surprising message from a Pope who himself lives simply and avoids all trappings of power.

Does your knowledge of Jorge Bergoglio predate back to before his election to the papacy? Was there a meeting or encounter between you that left a special memory?

No, I did not have the privilege of knowing him before his election. I have only spent some time with Jesuits in my country and in my training in EAPI.[1]

In the last 50 or 60 years, the figure of the pope has changed enormously, especially in the way people imagine it. Now Pope Francis is contributing a lot to this change. Some observers have spoken controversially of 'desacralisation' of the papacy. How would you respond to this criticism?

You put it rightly, 'some', since the majority of the world appreciates his approach. You are aware that millions have left the Church or even the faith in the last 50 years, and European countries have become secularized. Let's consider how this Pope is received by both the rich and the poor, how many thousands gather to listen to him, the warm reception of his *Evangelii Gaudium* and *Laudato si*, he has undoubtedly given a refreshing welcome and home to those who are groping for meaning.

The Church was started by a carpenter's son who was followed by fishermen and tax collectors. Those in the margins founded this Church without power or glory.

---

[1]   East Asian Pastoral Institute, based in Manila, Philippines, governed by the Society of Jesus.

Afterwards, for historical reasons, in Europe, the Church emerged powerful.

The universal warm reception this Pope receives is the evidence that the world wants a Church that is simple and in dialogue with the world, not only in words but by its own style. I think he has understood this message well.

Pope Francis, the first Pope from the Americas, has focused much attention on the 'peripheries'. Why is this significant?

Very simply, the Bible is a book that worries about the periphery. Starting from the Book of Exodus, Yahweh calls Moses with great words, 'I have witnessed the affliction of my people in Egypt' and 'I know well what they are suffering' (Ex 3:4). The Bible is consistent with its message of concern for the underdog.

Christ himself was to articulate his message through the Good Shepherd who goes in search of the lost sheep. He also affirmed that 'The Son of Man' came not to serve the healthy, but for the sick. The early Church was a counter-witness to the Greek-Roman world soaked in power games. The Church was a model of humanity. Then, slowly, it started to be corrupted by the power and money.

Can we consider Myanmar a 'periphery' for the Catholic Church? And if so, in what sense?

Myanmar is not just the periphery! It is the periphery of the peripheries! The people of Myanmar endured 60 years of inhumane dictatorship, in a country closed to the modern world for decades. Thousands became refugees and millions fled as migrant workers.

For the Catholic Church, it was an almost lethal blow. Missionaries were thrown out overnight, and all the Church properties, schools, hospitals were nationalized.

The dictators thought they had administered euthanasia to the Catholic Church. However, we refused to die. We were forgotten by the world, not even on the periphery. It was as though we were victims of amnesia, but not forgotten by Mother Church! Although we were unaware of this, truly Myanmar, the persecution, the little flock left to fend for itself, were in the minds of many popes!

We were the periphery of the peripheries, but in the core attention of God and the Church.

Francis's attention to those from faraway lands, what impact has it had on Asia? How has it even touched your own people, very much on 'the peripheries', in Myanmar?

Our people always love the popes. The attention of Pope Francis in particular has been a great honour to our people, who for such a long time were forced to walk in the darkness of hopelessness. Each Catholic of Myanmar feels the warmth of the Pope and the universal Church. At the consistory where I was appointed cardinal, they were so proud to see the Church of Myanmar raised to international attention, that many came to Rome on that occasion.

The government was surprised too. It was also, I think, secretly happy that their country, even if it is a traditionally and strongly Buddhist country, gained such attention. Both the government and the monks sent messages of appreciation. Now we see that we have been able to start a good work, at a national level, on peace-making and interreligious approaches to human problems.

Francis's messages about war (especially the 'piece-meal World War III', to which he often refers), the tragedies of migrants, the threats to the natural habitat preservation, always receive a lot of attention. What is the secret of the impact that Francis is always

able to receive, as if he were the voice of the conscience of humanity, beyond all borders?

'Catholic' Church means an 'universally' present Church. In this sense, the Vatican Council II amplified the Church's role in the world: 'The joys and the hopes, the sorrows and the anxieties of the man of this age, especially those who are poor or in any way suffering, these are the joys and hopes, the sorrows and anxieties of the followers of Christ.'[2] Our Pope speaks a universal language, reflecting the human quest of the people from all backgrounds. He reaches the ear of all. He speaks a simple language; he is a master in communicating, both in message and method.

The Church has been in the public square for a long time, but very often its language primarily spoke only to the elites and educated people. Pope Francis comes from the slums, he speaks the language of the world, really reflecting the pain, anguish and expectation of modern man and woman, especially the poor.

Pope Francis has opened a door as the first Pope from the Americas, and he is beloved. Has this reception perhaps opened a door for an Asian pope?

It is too early to speculate. The Church does not grow by quotas. It grows by its own charism, besides the fact that we strongly believe in the role of the Holy Spirit.

As a universal Church, we welcome everyone who reflects the message of Christ. Asia does have some charismatic churchmen. The next pope could be from Africa too. Only by having a universal outlook will the Catholic Church grow. Anyone with that *modus operandi* will be welcomed.

---

[2]   Vatican II, *Gaudium et Spes*, 1.

Asia is the only continent where Christianity has not experienced major growth. It is also the continent where Catholics suffer the most violent persecutions. The reasons are complex, but could you very briefly explain why it is so difficult for Christianity to enter into dialogue with the Asian spirit, namely its mentality and culture? Why does Christianity there often receive hostile treatment?

Asia is a confluence of great religions that predated Christ and Christianity. Hinduism is an ocean which is happy to assimilate any new stream into its vast spiritual corpus. A strong culture based on a different world view has spread very deep in the east. Buddhism has no god, and does not believe in changing religions.

The introduction of Christianity, unfortunately, came with colonization. In some countries, becoming a Christian means leaving the traditional culture and community. Most of the eastern religions insist on personal effort in salvation, recourse to contemplation, often deep silence, whereas Christianity, in many places, was introduced as belief in various dogmas.

Eastern religions insist on personal experience and a self-search. Christianity differs in its idiom. Recently much work is being done in interreligious dialogue and service as interreligious bodies.

Much has been said about the simplicity and sobriety of Pope Francis. This is evidenced in his choice of the very basic Ford Focus car, and in his residence at the guesthouse Santa Marta. Francis goes to great lengths to avoid being identified as a man of power, like the Popes of the past surrounded by their, one could say, 'papal court'. The world has met with favour this message, which however, on several occasions it seems

to have brought some confusion to the Church. In your opinion, is that true?

I can only talk about the people of Myanmar. I think people are very happy about a simple Pope who smiles a lot, embraces the poor and the disfigured, a Pope who speaks directly to their heart. Probably the rich countries may be worried about his stands about the market economy and his concern for global warming. In these two issues, the East stands to gain by Pope's stand on economic justice and environmental justice. I personally feel no confusion but a greater clarity about our mission to the margins.

The press welcomed with much fanfare Pope Francis's many gestures and words, which seemed surprising and new. Were you personally ever surprised by Francis?

There were many such occasions. I would single out his washing of the feet of the Muslim woman at Holy Thursday services. In one gesture, he knocked down two big walls. One wall was against the West's perception of Islam, and the second against the treatment of women. This of course was not well received by some who thought his kneeling in front of a Muslim woman diluted the grandeur of the papacy. We must remember, it was Jesus who knelt before His disciples, some betrayers, some who would abandon Him. The Church exists to serve. Service is power, to this Pope. This is a great message to me.

We similarly have encouraged dioceses to engage in similar acts in the parishes, I was happy to participate in a slum parish, washing the feet of Muslims and women.

The word mercy is the word that one could say sums up the meaning of Pope Francis's pontificate. In your opinion, why is Pope Francis so sensitive to this

theme? In Asian cultures, in general, do they know the concept of mercy?

In the fire and brimstone narrative of the Old Testament, the core message of mercy seems to have been forgotten. When Moses receives the Ten Commandments and asks Yahweh what he should say to the people, the Lord defines himself in this way, 'The Lord, the Lord God, compassionate and gracious, slow to anger, and abounding in loving kindness and truth' (Ex 34:6).

The Bible has two major themes in both the Old Testament and New Testament, compassion and mercy. I think this is a great moment in our faith history, when this Pope is focusing our attention on these two major attributes of God. In the Year of Mercy, Christians who once regarded Him as a frightening, punishing God began returning to a God who is more like the Good Shepherd in search of the lost sheep, and the Father who waits for his Prodigal Son to come home. These are poignant biblical themes, and the Year of Mercy was a great blessing.

These virtues are also the bedrock of eastern religions. Buddhism has two major commandments to its followers, *Karuna*, compassion or loving kindness, the same words used by Yahweh in the Book of Exodus, and *Metta*, that is mercy. These are the highest gifts a Buddhist can pray for, and are considered the two eyes of moral life.

For the press, Pope Francis is a very popular character. In fact, much of the press internationally devotes a great deal of attention to him. Is the Francis that the press reports the real Francis, the authentic one? Is there something that remains not said by media, in the shadows, something not really seen or heard?

I am not a media expert. You can see that the media frenzy is dying down, which is good. He is the Pope, the head of the Catholic Church. He cannot be a media favourite. Media can build and destroy. I think Pope Francis has a message that transcends media interest. I am only happy that the intense attention he has been getting is slowly declining.

Pope Francis's warnings against financial speculation, the globalization of indifference, the throwaway culture, the exploitation of the planet, have also resulted in some arguing he is an anti-capitalist Pope. What do you think about this accusation? Are there grounds for it?

I just think of Jesus, who gave the parable of the rich man and Lazarus. I think of His saying that it is easier for a camel to go through the eye of a needle than for someone who is rich to enter the kingdom of God. I think of His Sermon on the Mount: 'Blessed are the poor'

This world order is being built on injustice. Not just the Pope says this. Some of the most brilliant economists have said this, and that this status quo is not maintainable. The warped values on which capitalism is propped up today raise questions of the very survival of the human race.

Yes, Pope Francis has been criticized by the American business interest as 'anti-capitalist'. The Pope is a moral leader and he speaks to the world. On the other hand, capitalism needs to bring some self-regulation for its own survival. The crash of 2008 was brought about by its greed. I personally feel the Pope must raise these concerns even more dramatically and more often.

After two Synods on the Family, what has changed in practice? There are many different interpretations of *Amoris Laetitia*. In your opinion, where is the novelty, if there is one?

There are two worlds today. One world is the poor and constantly struggling. In those areas, the greatest concern is how to get food on the table, how to send the children to school, how to get out of the debt trap. There is also another world, a world not worried about hunger and poverty. It is worried about sexual preferences, same sex marriages, and so on.

I believe the document *Amoris Laetitia* affirms the traditional definition of marriage and its sacredness. Traditional communities, including Islamic communities, are aware that the destruction of family is the destruction of the society.

We are not seeking novelty from the Pope's documents. We are seeking discourses on justice. We are victims of economic injustice, environmental injustice. We are sad when we come to contact with the West and realize that the public debate is hijacked by groups whose agenda is not that of the poor.

Poverty to me is the biggest terrorism against the vulnerable. I do hope the Pope's energy remains focused on this.

Francis always repeats that at the essence of Christianity are the works of corporal mercy. He himself has made many significant gestures of solidarity by setting an example in the Vatican, in Rome and in his travels throughout Italy and around the world. Can it be said that, in this way, he has returned a bit of 'concreteness' to the Christian concept of human dignity?

Kindly read the Second Chapter of James, where the Apostle James is attacking faith that is sterile, without action. To be a Christian is to do good. For too long, we integrated the simple message of compassion of the carpenter's Son into exotic philosophical discourses and dogmas. Pope Francis brings back the method of Jesus: 'Be merciful as your heavenly Father is merciful' (Lk 6:36).

Religions in this beginning of the third millennium have again become a very important factor in international politics, the cultural debate, and many social phenomena. Very often, they have also become causes of conflict and division between people and cultures. From your point of view, as a cardinal coming from a country in which Catholicism is a small minority, is it possible to establish a dialogue between very different religions and cultures? Pope Francis, in this respect, expresses a very open, very confident approach. Is it a realistic attitude or not?

The conflicts mainly concern Abrahamic religions, but not the whole world is in conflict for religious reasons. I think it is necessary to distinguish between economic and religious reasons. For example, before 1971 there was no cold war in the Islamic world, then the invasion of Afghanistan extended it to those countries. It is a non-cultural conflict, which has begun especially for the resources in those countries. The war in Iraq was not a war of religion, but it has become one. I believe that a proper analysis of conflicts would explain many of the reasons that give rise to wars. Indonesia is the most populous Muslim country, but in that part of the world there are no conflicts. The Pope is confident and full of hope, because conflicts are not just a religious issue, although many extremists would like it to be so. The Pope follows the principles of the Gospel, he cannot preach hatred.

While on pilgrimage in the Holy Land in 2014, Pope Francis encouraged with different gestures and words interreligious dialogue, which for Asia is a crucial issue. There is a question in debate that for many years has animated the Catholic Church: does the interreligious dialogue come at the expense of evangeliza-

tion? In other words, if all religions are equally valid and all are on the same plane, why would Christians still need to proclaim Christ and the Gospel? What is your position in this debate?

This question could necessitate a big thesis paper. Pope St John Paul II in the document *Ecclesia in Asia* dealt with this issue. Christianity is an evangelizing religion. Every Christian has a task to proclaim the Gospel. Pope St John Paul II showed the way by saying that true proclamation starts with listening. Without listening to the other, even the good news becomes a contentious spark. Christianity has lot to contribute to the world. It starts with humility and respect, not the arrogance of earlier years. Thus, interreligious dialogue is very important.

3 CARDINAL TIMOTHY DOLAN
ARCHBISHOP OF NEW YORK

Humour and the Simplicity of Pope Francis

When did you meet Pope Francis for the first time? Did you have any impressions? What did you know about him?

I MET HIM FOR the first time when we began to assemble as cardinals after the resignation of Pope Benedict, the ten days of congregation meetings and prayer in preparation for the Conclave. I had never met him before, although I had heard a lot about him from my predecessor, Cardinal Edward Egan, who spoke very highly of him because he had worked closely with him at the 2001 Synod. Cardinal Egan served as the Synod's *General Relator*, and was extraordinarily impressed with Cardinal Bergoglio's depth, friendliness and desire to be of help. Cardinal Egan told me of the very heavy workload that he had, when at the end of the first day a very humble man came up and introduced himself as Jorge Bergoglio, Archbishop of Buenos Aires, and asked if he could be of any help. Cardinal Egan said, 'You bet you can', and Cardinal Bergoglio assisted him for the rest of the synod, and even took over his duties completely when Cardinal Egan came home early for the 9/11 Memorial Services. Even though I had often heard Cardinal Egan speak of him, I had never met Cardinal Bergoglio. I was a relatively new Cardinal at the time of the congregation meetings, so before and after the meetings I was trying to meet as many of my brother cardinals that I could. On a break I was getting a cup of coffee when I felt a tap on my shoulder. I turned around and he stuck out his hand and said, 'My name is Jorge Bergoglio. I think you are Timothy Dolan, and I wanted to meet you.' I was moved by his direct approach of wanting to meet me, and I was impressed with him from the beginning.

You and Pope Francis both have a great sense of humor; one can imagine there were some memorable exchanges between the two of you. Can you share with us maybe one or two such anecdotes?

Thanks for the compliment. I have two stories for you. I remember that he teased me from afar when we were in the midst of preparations for his pastoral visit to New York in 2015. Remember, he wanted to use a simple automobile, but he had told his person making the preparations to make sure that I could fit in the backseat of whatever car he used! I guess he knew that I was a man of girth, who could take a joke, and liked to tease on my own, so I immediately felt at home with him.

Then, at the conclusion of his effective and joyful visit to New York, when we were on the helicopter taking him to the airport to head to Philadelphia, he got himself a bottle of water and asked if I would like one too. I replied, 'Holy Father, as a matter of fact I would, I am very thirsty. I have not had much to drink these last 34 hours with you here because you never know when you can find a bathroom!' He laughed and said, 'I know what you mean. Haven't you had anything to drink?' I grinned and admitted, 'I will take a little drop of Jameson Whiskey.' He really laughed at that. A few minutes later, after we landed, and he was heading up the steps to the plane, I was the last one to shake his hand. He paused, turned to me, and said 'Have two drops of Jameson today to celebrate such a good visit!' He has a good sense of humor, and I would like to think I do as well, so we clicked.

You are the Archbishop of New York, a huge metropolis bringing together the various races, nations, levels of wealth, and so on. Cardinal Bergoglio lived almost the same experience in Buenos Aires. Do you see this past experience evidenced in the pontificate and teachings of Pope Francis?

Some people would claim that the transition from being Archbishop of Buenos Aires to Bishop of Rome and Pastor of the Universal Church must have been very difficult for him. From my perspective as the Archbishop of New York, which is very similar to being the Archbishop of Buenos Aires, I do not think it would have been a very tough transition at all. Like New York, Buenos Aires is a microcosm of the world. There is a mixture of the rich and poor, many ethnic groups, different languages, ongoing ecumenical and religious dialogues. I think all that prepared Cardinal Bergoglio to have the deftness, talent, experience, and finesse that he has shown as Pastor of the Universal Church.

What aspects of the teachings and pastoral approach of Pope Francis strike you the most?

As Pope, he is the supreme teacher of the Church, and he is faithfully passing on the substance of the faith, and so I do not see any difference from his predecessors in this regard. I do see a nuance in approach and style that I welcome. While I thank God for the approach and style of all the popes that I have known during my lifetime, I have seen Pope St John Paul II and Pope Benedict XVI more closely, and believe that their style and approach were most appropriate for them and most beneficial for the Church. Now Pope Francis has talents that we need today. No one can doubt that Pope Francis brings an amazing amount of simplicity, joy, and realism that helps me do my work here in New York. I am constantly stopped on the street by people from all backgrounds saying, 'Thank you for the gift of Pope Francis. We love him. He has inspired me to take a good hard look at my relationship with the Lord.' Those who are Catholics have said to me over and over again, 'I have drifted from the Church, but I like the Pope so much that I am taking a second look at the Church of my birth.' Those are extraordinary successes in his pontificate that would cause me as a fellow pastor to rejoice.

How is Pope Francis in private away from the cameras and press? What strikes you most about him as a man?

Well, to me, what you see is what you get. I find him to be very approachable, simple, and sincere. He does not try to impress, he does not want to talk all the time, and he enjoys asking a lot of questions. On the occasions that I have been with him, he has always asked a lot of questions about the Archdiocese of New York and about New York City. He seemed to be a man who was very at peace with himself, always taking everything in, watching and listening. To me, he seems to be the same in private as he is in public. I am glad he is.

How has he returned a bit of concreteness to the concept of human dignity, especially thinking of his efforts to help the marginalized, such as the poor, ill, migrants, human trafficking, and so on?

His teaching on the dignity of the human person and the sacredness of human life is as ringing and effective as those of Pope Benedict XVI and Pope St John Paul II, and Pope Francis adds very radiant examples. He realizes the power of presence. He realizes the efficacy of a symbol. What do I mean by that? Let me give you some examples. He goes to Lampedusa, he goes to a homeless shelter, and he washes the feet of young people in a facility for troubled youth.

These are all extraordinarily effective because they are just like Jesus, who always seemed to have a radar for those at the side of the road, who needed His blessing and embrace! That is what really gives teeth to his teachings on the dignity of the human person and sanctity of human life.

Another issue on which Pope Francis has had strong words and made significant gestures is the theme of immigration in the world today. He has repeated the invitation to build bridges and not walls. In your opinion, how far can you reach solidarity with migrants without the reception becoming unmanageable for a given nation or poor society?

Catholic teaching gives a nation the right to have secure borders, but is also clear that we have a moral imperative to welcome the immigrant. Pope Francis has been powerful in his teaching that the bias of any nation should be in favor of welcoming and helping people getting settled and that civilization depends on reaching out to the most vulnerable and the most in trouble. He is very sensitive to wherever human life is threatened, whether it be the baby in the womb, our elders, the starving, the war-torn, or persecuted Christians. He knows that the number of refugees and immigrants in the world today is bigger than the population of any country and he is very sensitive to them. He knows this is a real challenge to civilization, and that this planet that he loves so much cannot endure unless we all know that we have a responsibility to welcome those who are fleeing and seeking a better home, the immigrants and the refugees.

Pope Francis is loved and called the tweetable Pope, makes waves on social media and is very popular. You also are very popular, as you are the most followed Cardinal on Twitter. Do you think this popularity is

something the Pontiff seeks? Some say the Pope does not raise controversial issues in order to avoid criticism. What do you think about this suggestion?

What makes Pope Francis so incredibly popular is that he could not care less about being popular. He is who he is. He is sincere and authentic. He believes what the Bible says, that we need to please God and not human beings. He is not trying to court public opinion that enhances his popularity. I think he is amazed at how people love him. I could see he was moved by the exuberance with which hundreds of thousands of people greeted him in New York. He cannot understand why he is popular because becoming popular has never been his motive. He knows that Jesus cautioned us, 'Be careful when people speak well of you.' He just does what he feels called to do. I think people appreciate that, especially young people who can see through the facades of people who are trying to cultivate popularity.

You are Archbishop of New York, the Financial Capital, home to Wall Street. Pope Francis has said very strong words against idolatry of money and power. What do you think is correctly understood about his words on business and capitalism and what is not? Is he anti-capitalism?

His words about the dangers of riches are not any stronger than those of Jesus. Jesus is our model, the Supreme teacher, and Pope Francis does a good job articulating the teachings of Jesus and applying it to today when it comes to the danger of riches and wealth. What Pope Francis is really saying is traditional Catholic teaching, namely that money, wealth and property are not evil, but are morally neutral. It is the way we use them that matters. If they become our gods, our be-all and end-all, and if the accumulation of wealth at the expense of other people becomes our *modus operandi*, then that is immoral. Pope Francis is a very typical Catholic pastor, like his predecessors in saying that no one economic system is perfect. The Church traditionally has warned of the dangers of socialism and the dangers of unfettered capitalism. People here in the United States know that. Some of the best Catholics in New York work on Wall Street. They have seen the evils and the dangers of unrestricted capitalism. They have seen what happens when Wall Street runs wild, like in the movie, *The Wolf of Wall Street*. They do not want that. I think that thoughtful people know that Pope Francis is simply warning against excess on both sides.

The word mercy is the word one could say sums up Pope Francis's pontificate. In your opinion, why is Pope Francis so sensitive to this theme?

Pope Francis emphasizes mercy so frequently because he is so close to Jesus, and he knows that this was the preference of Jesus. He has such a strong sense of compassion for those who are trying their best to live up to what God expects of us, but who fail, as we all do. Pope Francis reminds us of that which is found throughout Sacred Scripture, in the psalms, in the Gospels. 'Neither do I condemn you. Go, and from now on do not sin any more' (Jn 8:11), as Jesus said to the woman caught in adultery.

Often Francis offers confessors advice. Is there one piece of advice in particular that you try to put into practice?

Pope Francis tells us the job description of a good confessor is to assure people of the mercy of Jesus, and not to lecture, criticize, or judge those who come before us. We priests realize that to be the case. Now sometimes a confessor might be asked by a penitent to help him or her judge an action, and that is fine. However, we priests always remember that when people come to confession the presumption is that they are sorry. They realize they are sinners and that is why they are there! They do not need us to add to their burden of guilt. What they need is for us to assure them that Jesus liberates them from their sin. That piece of advice helps me in my own pastoral role as a confessor.

After two Synods on the Family, what has changed in practice?

Pope Francis has not changed any teaching; he has reminded us, or maybe affirmed, the traditional ways that the Church has always offered to help people in delicate situations, namely the invitation to seek the declaration of nullity and for tribunals to work with people to expedite that procedure. That is a good thing that all parish priests would applaud. Secondly, he has urged us pastors to make certain that individuals or couples in particularly difficult situations use their conscience in accord with Church Teaching when making decisions about their relationship with Jesus and the sacramental life of the Church. So once again it is not a question of a change in Doctrine or our deeply held moral belief that comes to us from the Bible, it is a question of how we help people live it.

Turning to *Amoris Laetitia* there are many interpretations, do you think this document is causing confusion or is it clear? Is this just an example of the Church using non-condemning language or does it represent concrete change?

I would share the frustration of Pope Francis that people seem to concentrate on a tiny section of *Amoris Laetitia* and forget the overwhelming teaching of that document, namely that the sacrament of marriage, the vocation of marriage, is under tremendous challenge today. The Church is at her best when she restores the luster, the beauty, the romance, the nobility of life-long, faithful, life-giving, loving marriage. What the Church does best and the Synod reaffirmed, is what the Pope does in *Amoris Laetitia* as he speaks about the challenge to marriage and family life. I would share his frustration that these delicate, neuralgic issues seem to get a lot more attention than the overwhelmingly positive reaffirmation of the magnificence of God's plan for marriage, the urgency of sound preparation of couples for marriage, and the encouragement we are summoned to provide our couples striving to be faithful.

Francis's warnings against financial speculations, the globalization of indifference, the throw away culture are always making headlines, yet Francis's teachings on the themes of family, marriage, defence of life, do not have the same impact. In your opinion, why is this?

That would not be unique to Pope Francis. We always prefer to cherry-pick; when the Pope says something we like, we applaud, and when the Pope says something we do not like or do not agree with, we try to wiggle out of it. He is a good pastor and teacher. Every pastor, every preacher, can sympathize with him because we all get criticized when we say something that people do not want to hear, just as we all get applauded when we say something with which others might agree or want to hear. All you can do is continue to preach the Gospel, articulate the Truth with love, as Pope Francis does.

Pope Francis is not always clearly understood on sensitive themes. You too have shown a welcoming to all people if they do not live their life in accordance with Church Teaching, for example I think of gay

couples, but likewise you do not condone. While you always welcome, you do not compromise on Church Teaching. Given your experience, how do you think Francis keeps this balance of mercy and openness to all but at the same time not touching Doctrine?

Once again, I think of the example of Jesus. When we think of the Catholic Church, we know 'all are welcome.' We cannot stop there though, as we ask, 'all are welcome' to what? All are welcome to a community of sinners who are trying, with the grace and mercy of God, to be saints, to conform their lives to what God has revealed. All are welcome to a community that is trying to help one another live up to the high moral imperatives of Jesus. So, on the one hand we say, 'Come on in, you are welcome,' and on the other hand, 'You are welcome' to a community that is trying its best to fight sin and to grow in grace.

During his pontificate, what has surprised you most about this Pope or when has he surprised you the most?

My pleasant surprise is that he has continued after almost four years to capture the world's fascination and imagination which is very much needed. As a pastor in Milwaukee and now in New York, it would make me bristle that people immediately would think the worst about the Church and never give the Church a chance. Many people seem to have a caricature of the Church, the stereotype that it is stern, nay-saying, and unwelcoming. We knew that was not the case; we knew, in fact, that the exact opposite was true under John Paul and Benedict. With his refreshing openness, Pope Francis is chipping away at that caricature. I thank God for the fact that people are still fascinated, listening to him, and intrigued by him, after almost four years. For that I thank God, because many more people are now open to the message of Jesus as faithfully preached by His Church.

One can say that Pope Francis at his consistory has named cardinals truly from the peripheries, even from very small nations where Christianity is in the minority. What criteria do you believe are behind his decisions?

We say the Church is One, Holy, Catholic, and Apostolic. Pope Francis is really heavy on the catholicity, the fact that the Church is 'universal'. To be Catholic means, as the Irish writer James Joyce said, 'Here comes everybody.' That is what Pope Francis wants to show. One way he can do that is in the make-up of the College of Cardinals. Cardinals just do not come from North America or from Europe. Cardinals can come from far-off ocean islands, and from little countries. Now we even have a Cardinal in Newark which is right across the Hudson River. New Yorkers might think it is foreign territory, but I am glad to have a brother Cardinal so close by.

The press considers Pope Ratzinger and Pope Bergoglio to be two very different personalities, but in this undeniable diversity, in your opinion is there something that unites them?

What unites them most closely is a fidelity to the Truth, a passion for Jesus and His Church. In his undeniable love and tender embrace of Pope Benedict, Pope Francis shows us his respect and admiration for his predecessor. I would bet that Pope Francis would be the first to admit that Pope Benedict had a sense of scholarship and erudition that all of us would love to have, himself included. Pope Francis, while himself an extraordinarily intelligent, educated, and well-read man, also knows that his *forte* rests more on human, relational warmth, but that does not mean that there is any difference at all in substance between Pope Benedict and Pope Francis.

Religions in the beginning of this third millennium have again become a very important factor in international politics, the cultural debate and many other social phenomena. Very often as in the past they have also become the cause of conflict and division between people and cultures. Is it possible to establish a dialogue between very different religions and cultures? Pope Francis, in this respect, expresses a very open, very confident approach. Is it a realistic attitude or not?

It is very realistic and he is showing us that it is. To me, one of the great contributions of Pope Francis is that he is succeeding in shattering the caricature of religion as a cause of division, violence, and misunderstanding in the world. We believers know that religion, faith, the Church, is a source of affirmation, enhancing everything that is good, decent, noble, and loving in the human project. Religion is the source of unity, never division. Religion is the source of love, never hate. Religion brings people together, never divides them. The world would have us believe otherwise. Pope Francis is showing us the genuine definition of religion, namely, as the home of faith, hope and love and bringing people together.

Pope Francis is the first Pope from the Americas. Do you think his nomination would represent an opening of a door for a North American Pope?

People still ask me, 'Do you think we will ever have an American Pope?' I always reply, 'We have one and I am proud of him!' We in the United States sometimes arrogantly identify America with the United States, when really, we are only a part of it. I think it is clear after the election of Karol Wojtyla, Joseph Ratzinger and Jorge Bergoglio that the Bishop of Rome can come from anywhere.

What do you think Pope Francis thinks about the Church in the United States? Has he ever shared his thoughts on New Yorkers or New York?

He shared with me while he was here, albeit for a short time, that he was overwhelmingly impressed with the outreach of our Catholic charities, with the effectiveness of our Catholic schools, particularly in educating the poor, with the generosity of our people, the diversity of our ethnic identity, and the vitality of our faith. I think that is a pretty darn good report card.

Is there advice that Pope Francis has given that you use to guide New York's faithful? Is there some way he has inspired you in your ministry?

He has affirmed some of the hunches I have had for a long time, namely that you can never go wrong in being with people; that joy is the infallible sign of God's presence, that without prayer and faith anything we do is useless. The Holy Father also affirmed that we need to be a light to the world, that we do not need a lot of clutter, pomp, and excess to do our work of serving God's people.

4 ARCHBISHOP GEORG GÄNSWEIN

PREFECT OF THE PAPAL HOUSEHOLD & PERSONAL SECRETARY OF POPE EMERITUS BENEDICT XVI

Pope Emeritus Benedict, a Wise Grandfather at Home

Two Popes living in the Vatican is truly an unusual situation. However, it seems very natural to both Pope Francis and Pope Emeritus Benedict XVI. Is it as natural as it appears?

I T TRULY IS. This is not my personal opinion, it is true. From the beginning, it was obvious to all on 28 June 2016, at the 65th anniversary of the priestly ordination of the Pope Emeritus. Francis spoke to the cardinals about Benedict, and Benedict concluded with thanking Francis. During the ceremony, one could see and feel the admiration and respect they have for each other.

In your opinion, what is the secret of this naturalness?

The naturalness comes from a reciprocal esteem, mutual admiration, and respect. I witness it daily; it is not a façade, it is genuine. If it were only a façade, the sincerity would not be felt by others.

At the beginning, when Pope Benedict XVI announced his resignation, many looked ahead with concern at the situation that would be created. Thinking back to that time, do you think there were legitimate reasons for this worry?

The resignation of Pope Benedict was an unprecedented, unexpected act. For many, including myself, it was almost unthinkable. After the resignation, one was looking ahead to the conclave of electing a new pope. Benedict became the 'Pope Emeritus'. He stated clearly that he was no longer the Pope, no longer involved in governing the Church, but here to pray for the Church and for his successor.

Here I believe that the disbelief of some was greater than trust in the future. I understand this uncertainty and it is human. However, with the passing of time, one could see these worries were unfounded.

The Pope Emeritus and Pope Francis are considered to be very different. You know both up close: what do they share in common or what unites them?

You are right. From the outside; they could appear as two different personalities, in styles, gifts, human and Church experiences, in their biographies and in their way of governing. It is not something at which to marvel. What they share in common is the same faith in Christ, the same love for the Lord and the Church that is evident in their daily lives.

What would you say is the greatest difference between them?

A notable difference between the two that one notices right away is the way they relate to the people, that is their approach. Pope Francis has an incredibly direct approach towards people. The Pope Emeritus is a person who slowly approaches others. They are very different from this point of view. This is simply a part of the personality, simply in their DNA.

The wording of their Teachings differs. Pope Benedict spoke of reason and relativism. Pope Francis speaks of mercy and tenderness. Is it only a change of language and emphasis or something more?

Every pope, when elected, finds himself in front of realities that require an immediate response. The challenges when Benedict XVI was elected Pope were different with respect to the challenges Francis has to confront today. That is to say that for all the popes and every pope, on the basis of their personal experiences and convictions; they develop the principal points that characterize their governing. You mentioned two key words, 'reason' and 'relativism,' for Pope Benedict XVI, and 'tenderness' and 'mercy' for Pope Francis. In fact, they are keywords for both Popes, not exclusive to just one of them. Otherwise one goes off course and does not welcome the totality and completeness of their message. Obviously, also a different sensibility influences both the way and the content of the teaching.

Is there a particular challenge to which you refer?

The real challenge that arises under different facades is the challenge of faith. It is important to say that the pope must confirm his brothers in the faith and must announce the Word of the Lord, appropriately, in order that the faithful feel confirmed and sustained. Meeting this challenge is the priority and remains incredibly timely.

The press often 'exalts' Pope Francis, but they were often less tender with Pope Benedict XVI. Do you have an explanation for this?

It is obvious and everyone can see that the mass media are very favorable when it comes to Pope Francis, much more than toward his predecessor. One does not need to give this too much significance. The mass media are not the measure of the works of the successor of Peter. I believe that this question also regards the way one communicates. Francis is a man who knows how to communicate and also does so with surprises and unexpected gestures, which for mass media are easy to transmit. With regard to Benedict, his great gift was the written word and preaching, not as much the gestures. To listen requires patience and commitment. However, it is true that media are an important reality in announcing the Gospel and it is necessary to communicate the truths of the faith in a simple, understandable, and convincing way, attracting the attention of the modern world with gestures. With this, we see Pope Francis has a special gift.

Francis has innovated a lot the style of the pope, modifying many customs. He has made us understand he does not care much for formalities. In your opinion, what are these changes causing people to think?

Every pope, every man, has his way of being, his personal style. It is true that Pope Francis has changed some things. His predecessors did the same thing, even if not as quickly, but more slowly and gradually. The protocol and the *stilus curiae* are neither a corset nor an intolerable armour for the successor of Peter, but the fruit of much experience gathered throughout the centuries that then becomes rules that help the pope confront the numerous daily commitments. Seen up close, the changes of which you speak are not radical changes. It is absolutely normal and legitimate to update habits and customs.

Is there a certain change that struck or surprised you the most?

The choice to live in Santa Marta truly surprised me. As the private secretary of Benedict XVI, I lived in the Apostolic

Palace and this experience was very positive especially with respect to daily life of the Pope with numerous audiences and encounters. In the meantime, we have gotten used to the new situation. That is to say at the beginning it could have appeared very surprising or unusual, but now it has become normal and part of daily life.

Someone has commented, negatively, about the assumed excessive freedom of Francis, the spontaneity of his many attitudes. To those who speak of a 'desacralisation' of the Papacy, what do you respond?

I do not share this opinion. To speak of the 'desacralisation' of the Papacy is misleading. Changes of protocol are not a sin. It is not a drama. There is nothing to object. To give an example, there was a protocol change for when he welcomes heads of State in the Vatican. The Pope always used to put on the *mozzetta* [the shoulder-length cape of red velvet trimmed with white fur] and the stole too, in case of a Catholic Head of State. Pope Francis, instead, does not wear these. The night of the election, appearing on the Loggia of the Blessings, he did not want to wear these. It was a personal choice, his decision.

During this pontificate, we have witnessed surprising episodes. You already spoke of Francis's decision to live at Santa Marta, but when did you feel most surprised by Pope Francis?

In addition to Santa Marta, one must also remember that quickly an idea spread which did not correspond to Francis's reasons for choosing Santa Marta. Many had assumed that Francis did not want to live in the pontifical apartment because it was too luxurious and lavish. The Pope himself reiterated that the papal apartment is neither luxurious nor lavish, but is too big for him. He is not used to a lot of space, and therefore, preferred to live in Santa Marta. This he has said many times, but unfortunately a false idea has been created which is hard to dispel. Anyway, Pope Francis is a person who surprises and welcomes surprises. The surprises make up part of his pontificate. For me as Prefect of the Papal Household, we try to help the Pope to put into practice the surprises requested by him.

Turning to the resignation of Pope Benedict XVI, Francis has said many times, that it was an 'open door'. Do you believe that in the future a Pope will repeat that decision?

Yes, Benedict XVI opened a door. Many times, Pope Francis returned to this point and spoke of the Pope Emeritus demonstrating understanding and appreciation for his courageous decision. However, it is not, and it is important to underline, automatic! It must be a free decision taken in conscious in front of the Lord. If it were not, it would neither be valid.

In the past, Pope Francis had said in the future he also could be open to this possibility?

It is clear that often journalists listen to a word, often out of context, and construct a variety of interpretations. It is necessary to distinguish between that which the Pope effectively says and that which is the fruit of journalistic interpretations, and possible manipulations.

Are there risks though that the pontificate could become a fixed-term office?

No, I am convinced it is not and will not be so. If someone thinks that Pope Benedict has resigned with this purpose, he does not understand fully the choice of Benedict, nor appreciate its value. If a pope is convinced that he can no longer continue, it is legitimate for him to renounce the Petrine Ministry out of love for the Lord and the Church. It is a very courageous act and one of great humility.

Everyone says that Pope Francis often demonstrates an unpredictable sense of humour.

Pope Francis has a great sense of humour. He uses it and obviously is happy if the recipient appreciates. I must add that Pope Benedict has a great sense of humour. Humour is a medicine and it has a great human value. It helps to live better.

How often does it happen that you comment with Benedict XVI episodes or gestures of this pontificate?

Often, I tell at home how private and other encounters and audiences go during the day. Pope Benedict listens but does comment. He is interested in various anecdotes but it is not his style to comment.

Many commentators emphasize the idea of change or revolution that Francis would have carried with him. What are rather, in your opinion, the elements of continuity with Benedict XVI?

One must distinguish between the content and the personal style. To do the same thing in a different way does not at all mean to change its contents. In some journalistic narrations or those done by various commentators, more or less improvised, they tend to misrepresent the reality. They confuse the personal style with changing the contents. In some cases, some force seeks a change or novelty even if there is not. With regard to the Teachings of his predecessors, one must observe a single realty without any exception. There is a persistent continuity with regard to the Teachings of his predecessors. Between the Teachings of Benedict and of Francis, I see no difference. I would like to underline the approaches are diverse, but absolutely not in the substance.

You were witness to various encounters between Francis and Benedict. Can you tell us an episode or detail that moved you?

What really moved me and continues to do so is the goodness of Pope Francis toward Benedict. Already in the first encounter of 23 March 2013, ten days after his election, this great goodness from the heart of the new pope towards his predecessor was perceptible. Moreover, each time, when Francis visits Benedict at the *Mater Ecclesiae* monastery in the Vatican where he lives, I witness this. For the occasion of his 65th anniversary of priestly ordination, Benedict himself spoke of the goodness of Pope Francis toward him using a very touching expression, namely that the goodness of Francis toward him is more beautiful than the beauty of the Vatican Gardens.

And Pope Francis? I imagine that he sometimes speaks of Benedict XVI. If the question is not too impertinent, could you tell us something? One time, Francis said to have Pope Benedict in the Vatican is like having 'a wise grandfather at home.' In what sense, was the Pope affirming this?

The first time that Pope Francis used the phrase that you cited, it was during an encounter with journalists on a flight returning from an international visit. I was at Rome's Ciampino Airport waiting to welcome him. Exiting the flight, coming down the stairs, before even greeting each other he tells me, 'Today, I said something a little strong. I spoke of Pope Benedict as a wise grandfather at home! I hope he is not offended.' By all means no! It is a lovely image, perhaps a bit surprising coming from the mouth of the Pope, but sincere and said with great sentiments, affection, and conviction. It is a strong immediate, sincere, and beautiful image, coherent with the style of Pope Francis. Furthermore, thinking of the spiritual richness of Benedict XVI, it is not absurd to recognize him like a grandfather rich of experience and wisdom.

5 CARDINAL KURT KOCH

PRESIDENT OF THE PONTIFICAL COUNCIL FOR PROMOTING CHRISTIAN UNITY

Pope Francis Parish Priest of the Universal Church

On 13 March 2013, in St. Peter's Square, Pope Francis, just elected, presented himself as 'Bishop of Rome', rather than 'Pope'. What value did this choice of words convey to other churches and Christian denominations?

FIRST, I WOULD say, it is not new. The Pope is the 'Bishop of Rome'. Pope St John Paul II took this title very seriously, visiting a Roman parish when he had a free Sunday, as did Benedict XVI. Therefore, more than being something new, it is in continuity. Its importance for the relations with the other churches is clear, the Orthodox churches in particular, as they follow a *taxis*, in other words 'an order' of the sees with Rome and its bishop in the first place up to the Schism of 1054, then Constantinople, Alexandria, Antioch and Jerusalem. Yes, today is a good sign if the Pope calls himself 'Bishop of Rome'.

Did you already know Cardinal Bergoglio before his election as Pope?

I had heard something reported about the Buenos Aires Archbishop. I never met him until the week before the Conclave of 2013, during the congregation meetings at the Paul VI Hall. The cardinals gathered to discuss the situation of the Church in all the five continents. Our first meeting happened, when he gave his important speech.

Among all your 'routine' meetings, is there one that left a stronger impression?

Every meeting with the Holy Father is special, because Francis is deeply interested in ecumenism. He desires to develop it more and more. The audiences to representatives of other Churches and ecclesial communities I attended have been particularly beautiful. I fondly remember, for example, the audience in the Apostolic Palace to the representatives of the Valdese community. It was a very warm, good and encouraging encounter. Even when the issues are very serious, Pope Francis conveys his sharp sense of humour.

You have taken part in many encounters between the Pope and known Christian figures. As a privileged witness, what could you say is the most impressive side of Francis for the non-Catholics?

His credibility is expressed by the sense of brotherhood and friendship he shows: the emphasis he always put on the importance of the mutual recognition of our baptism; the stress he lays on our journeying together towards unity. The reaction that I observe is joy, especially for understanding that we are really brothers.

The figure of the Pope has changed a lot in the last 50 or 60 years, also thanks to Pope Francis. Some say that the papacy has been 'desacralised'. What are your thoughts and what do you think could be the effect on ecumenical dialogue?

I do not see with Francis great changes on this point. I see rather great continuity. From the beginning of his pontificate, Pope Francis declared that he would follow the footsteps of his predecessors from the Vatican Council II up to today. This has been repeatedly confirmed, for example, at the celebration of the Vespers in the St. Paul Outside the Walls Basilica, in Rome, at the end of the Week of Prayer for Christian Unity. Francis has declared continuity with predecessors; Blessed Paul VI, St John Paul II, and Benedict XVI. Certainly, it is obvious, compared to them he is another person. Each Pope is different from the other. Let's consider, in particular, Benedict XVI and his announcement of resignation. It has been a great sign for many other churches. According to Francis, to be open to other churches means first of all brotherhood and closeness. After his election as Pope, I remember, I met him and asked what he would desire for the ecumenism. He replied with only one word, 'brotherhood.'

Looking at Pope Francis' Magisterium and pastoral style, what elements would you say are most evident?

I would underline three 'dimensions' of Francis's pontificate and Magisterium. The first is the pastoral dimension. The Holy Father considers himself the shepherd to whom is entrusted the care of the souls, the parish priest of the universe. He searches always for the direct contact with the others, because he takes care of their joys and their suffering. The second is the prophetic dimension. Pope Francis demonstrates clarity and perspicacity calling by name the big challenges the Church must face in society today. He is concerned especially for the excluded people, in terms both geographic and existential. Finally, there is the spiritual dimension. He is a man of deep faith, who feeds his life and his work with the Gospel. These three dimensions explain very well why he is perceived as an absolutely genuine person by so many people, as well as those outside the Church.

The press strongly welcomed many gestures and words of the Pope that seemed surprising and new, not only in regards to the ecumenism. On what occasion did you feel most surprised by Francis?

Francis's gestures have a particularly important role. They give him the opportunity to express, in an ever more incisive way, the concept he wants to express. From this perspective he reveals a clear similarity and proximity to Paul VI, the Pope who did make prophetic gestures for the ecumenism. Anyway, Francis always surprises me when he doesn't hesitate to admit the mistakes of the Church. He asks forgiveness from the representatives of other churches and denominations; such as Valdese, Lutheran, Pentecostal, regretting everything that has been done against them.

There have been other surprising circumstances, too, when Francis has denounced more or less openly some flaws or wrong attitudes that are diffused around the Vatican. You have been part of the Roman Curia for several years. How do you accept this criticism?

The first time he spoke really openly on these problems was the traditional audience to the Roman Curia before Christmas. Now, we need to understand why the Holy Father chose that audience to raise them. First of all, he could have thought, all the members of the Roman Curia go to confess, surely. Maybe he said to himself, 'I want to compile a list of all the potential sins that could be committed' [Cardinal Koch smiles], as if that audience were a sort of examination of conscience before the confession. Only from this spiritual 'perspective' you must read what the Pope said. He added that these mistakes or sins are not a privilege of the Curia members but of all Christian people.

Pope Francis very often has made us understand that the core of ecumenism, according to him, is not the dialogue on theological or doctrinal issues. Francis does not seem to have many concrete expectations from theologians. Did you ever get the same impression, hearing from him that 'the theologians will never reach an agreement', or something similar?

There is always a bit of humour when the Holy Father speaks about theologians, because there is really a risk that the theologians want to know, define, and discuss endlessly all the questions. It is clear, even for Francis; the theological dialogue has its importance for the ecumenism. It is not the foundation. The foundation is love. We need a distinction between ecumenism of truth and ecumenism of love. The first foundation of the ecumenism is a friendly and fraternal relationship between different churches. The second is the 'practical' ecumenism, not less important in the Pope's opinion. It means in working together all is possible for us at a cultural, social and political level, especially evangelizing together. The division between the churches is the largest obstacle for the announcement of the Gospel. Let us rediscover the unity, so we will have a more credible message to announce, this is very much at the heart of the Pope.

Therefore, the theological dialogue must be considered a commitment among various others, but not the 'only' commitment. As Francis often says, ecumenism is created on the path. To walk together means already to create unity.

Certainly, Francis is used to attributing more value to gestures than to words. I remember the encounter with Kirill in Cuba, when the Holy Father and the Patriarch of Russia signed a solemn, common declaration. The Pope clarified a few times after having

signed it, it was only a 'pastoral' declaration. Since some did not like these words, could you explain what it should mean?

Let's begin saying that obviously the encounter was really more important than the declaration. Namely the fact that such a very much anticipated encounter could finally happen in Cuba. On the other hand, if Francis and Kirill had not signed any declaration, people could have asked, 'Why did they meet? What did they discuss? What did they want to say each other?' So, it has been necessary to create a common declaration. Now, it must be understood too that if you sign a 'common' declaration, the content can't be the 100% of what you would like to declare, from your side only. I mean whatever speech the Pope gives, he is free to say all he intends to say. In a common declaration, you must verify first of all what can be said together and what cannot be said. To draw up a solemn common declaration to sign after a meeting that happens the first time in history, is not easy!

I believe, the declaration demanded being read without starting out with a negative prejudice, rather with having a positive predisposition to gather how much good has been said. Certainly, we could not ignore the very strong reactions of some orthodox sectors from Russia, blaming the Patriarch Kirill, nor the reactions from the Ukrainian, Greek Catholics. I think that many accusations were indeed misunderstandings to clarify, because the Ukrainian Greek Catholic Church is very close to the Pope's heart.

After a long period without relations between the Catholic and Russian Orthodox Churches, the world's two largest Churches in terms of numbers baptised, there was this greatly anticipated encounter, a milestone ecumenically. Why has this taken so long,

especially given that both John Paul II and Benedict XVI desired a rapprochement with the Russian Orthodox Church, but did not succeed?

Yes, it is well known, even Pope St John Paul II nourished a strong desire to meet the Orthodox Patriarch of Russia. It was not long before this meeting happened. It had been scheduled on the occasion of the second European Ecumenical Conference in Graz, Austria, in 1997. Everything was ready, but at the last minute, Moscow cancelled it, because of problems between the two Churches.

Benedict XVI, had also desired an encounter with the Patriarch Kirill, since he already knew him very well as metropolitan Archbishop, before Kirill became Patriarch. However, the Patriarch didn't think the times were right. Finally, some years later, the meeting happened in Cuba, with Pope Francis. Undoubtedly, the fact that Francis expressed with clear determination his wish to meet the Patriarch, without laying any conditions, was a great contribution. On the other side, the Patriarch agreed that such an encounter was necessary, especially in the light of the world situation today and the cruel persecutions against the Christians. We are all deeply grateful for the occurrence of this event. I would have been glad also if the meeting had happened with Pope Benedict XVI if he had not resigned. I repeat, the insistence of Pope Francis has been a great help. I remember what he said on the plane returning to Rome from Constantinople: namely, in substance, 'I will meet the Patriarch. He could say when and where and I will be there.' Yes, this availability has helped very much.

The Protestant Reformation, started by Luther, is 500 years old. Today the distance between Rome and Protestantism is surely greater than with the Ortho-

dox. Has the celebration of this anniversary been useful, in some way, to reduce these distances?

Relative to the faith, yes, certainly we have more in common with the Orthodox than with the Protestants. It is also true that we have been able to rediscover a lot of common beliefs with Protestants, through the intense dialogue of the last 50 years. For example, for the first time in the history an anniversary of the Reformation has been celebrated together, in a spirit of ecumenical communion, with a participation of Catholic representatives. It has been a great opportunity to take, in order to make new steps on the path of this so desired unity. Pope Francis, as you know, has taken part in the joint commemoration of the Reformation on 31 October 2016 in Lund, Sweden, presiding at the liturgical service together with the President and the General Secretary of the World Lutheran Federation. This event has been a very meaningful sign of reconciliation.

There were three points on the Lund agenda. The first one was 'gratitude', because 2017 marks not only 500 years of the Reformation, but also 50 years from the beginning of the Catholic-Lutheran dialogue; a long period, during which we discovered many common things. This is gratitude! The next point is 'repentance', because after the Reformation we experienced divisions and also horrible religious wars in the XVI and XVII centuries. We really must do penance for these wars we fought. Today it's very important to discuss this matter, thinking to the wars inside the Islamic world. Nevertheless, we must also recognize that Catholics and Lutherans did the same thing. So, let's repent! Finally, 'hope', the third point, hope that such a celebration will help us to open new good perspectives for our dialogue.

Speaking of Lutherans, recently Pope Francis provoked some controversy when he expressed that Luther was a reformer prompted by intentions that 'were not wrong.' What do you believe Francis intended to say?

While addressing the statement to which you refer, Pope Francis surely had in mind the fundamental purpose of Martin Luther, namely to not produce divisions of the Church, nor to find a new church. His purpose was to renew the Catholic Church starting from the Gospel. The heart of Luther's thought and work was the rediscovery of the evangelical message of the justification of sinners not by the works of men, but only by grace of God.

Then 'that necessary' reform of the Church resulted in another reform, leading the Church itself to division. It is one of the most tragic pages of history of the Church. Now we are committed, in ecumenical communion, to overcome it.

Ecumenism is really a complex matter, with many different implications. It's easy to argue the 'average' Christian man or woman has not done comprehensive theological nor ecumenical historical studies and does not have in-depth wide knowledge of it. Nevertheless, they would see some concrete and valuable progress. Do you perceive such progress ahead, even maybe celebrating Easter on the same date?

The objective you point to would be a very significant point for the ecumenism, to set a common date for the celebration of the Easter, especially for the cases of mixed marriage between different Christian denominations. In fact, now the husband could tell the wife, 'My Lord is already risen. When will your Lord rise?' [he laughs]. As we know, the Orthodox churches follow different calendars; unfortunately, there is not an easy solution to this problem. I was hoping that at the Pan-Orthodox Synod of Crete, June 2016, a solution could be adopted at least by all the Orthodox churches. This point was not put on the synod-agenda. If an agreement is so difficult to define even among the Orthodox churches; setting a common date valid for all the Christian denominations becomes more difficult. However, Pope Francis has a very strong desire to find common dates to celebrate Christian solemnity. The contribution of the Coptic-Orthodox Egyptian Patriarch, Tawadros II is also a great help.

Although it seems so difficult to believe, today in Europe there are still wars where even divisions among different Christian churches come into play. Ukraine is a clear example. What should be done in order to prevent the exploitation of religion to pursue non-religious interests?

In Ukraine today, the fundamental point for the Christian churches is how to be part of the solution, rather than of the problem. I think that the history has left too many wounds, on both the sides. Therefore, I really believe on the importance of the 'purification of the memory', that Pope St John Paul II often spoke about; it means to elaborate a common historical vision. This purification could provide a big help to restore a greater unity.

Let us consider, as an example, the Francis proposal regarding another controversy, in Serbia between Catholic and Orthodox Churches, the canonization cause of the Croatian Cardinal Aloysius Stepinac, the Archbishop of Zagreb during the Second World War. Since the Serbian Orthodox raised several problems around Cardinal Stepinac, the Holy Father proposed to carry out an historical research, to review all the information and to find a solution. This proposal goes exactly in the direction just mentioned. The same process perhaps would be useful and necessary in the Ukrainian situation today.

Pope Francis and Ecumenical Patriarch of Constantinople Bartholomew, show a mutual understanding based on a strong, personal friendship. You have observed this up close, do you have any anecdotes to share?

This is evidence that the personal friendship between religious leaders is a big help along the ecumenical path, because on this ground they can resolve many problems. In addition to this, we already have the great tradition of the reciprocal visits to Rome and Constantinople. Every year, a delegation comes from Constantinople to Rome to celebrate our patrons Saints Peter and Paul, on the 29 June. Another delegation from Rome goes to Constantinople to celebrate St Andrew, on 30 November. Finally, I like particularly to remember a conversation they had during a lunch. Bartholomew, you must know, spent in Rome a period as a student, several years ago. He said, 'when I am in Rome, I always go to enjoy a nice cappuccino.' Then the Pope answered: 'You can still do that, but I no longer can.' The Patriarch said, 'we can go together!'

On 16 April 2016, Francis and Bartholomew decided to visit the Middle Eastern refugees on the Greek Island of Lesbos. Today's great tragedies seem to bring together Catholic, Protestants, and Orthodox communities. To what extent, though, can different doctrinal views, especially tied to family and life, be ignored?

It is also important to remember that present in Lesbos was the Orthodox Archbishop of Athens, Ieronymos II. I

think that similar gestures, as in Lesbos, are truly significant with regard to the purpose of offering to the world a
common witness on behalf of any human being. The
human being is the core of the faith and the action of all
the Christian people. I would say that everything we can
do together, we must do. It will become a beautiful
evidence that Christian people, even if divided into different churches or communities, take the same care of each
man and of the whole humanity.

Having said this, even after events like Lesbos the theological problems remain unresolved. This is another order
of issues. We must continue to reflect on them. My opinion
on the examples you mentioned, the Magisterium of the
different churches on themes related to family, life, and so
on, is that they constitute a reason to be very worried.

The reality is that in recent times new tensions came
to the surface on the ecumenical relations, especially in
the field of ethical issues. They represent a relevant
difference, in comparison with past ages, when according
to the common opinion; the faith divided while the acts
united. Today we must admit, the situation is just the
opposite. Now there is a solid consensus reachable on
many issues related to faith, but there is also sharp
disagreement about some ethical problems like those
concerning the human life and its beginning and its end,
the marriage, the family, sexuality, gender. The ecumenical
dialogue must go more and more into them, because it is
important, in our society today, to speak up clearly, as
Christians, with one voice, agreeing with each other on
decisive issues, regarding human life and social cohabita-
tion. Otherwise, if we are unable to speak up with only one
united voice on fundamental issues of the humanity today,
our single voices will become increasingly weak. This is
an enormous challenge too, nowadays, for the ecumenism.

There is a famous declaration of the encyclical letter *Ut unum sint* (1995), namely Pope St John Paul II's openness to find a new way of exercising the Petrine primacy, to facilitate the ecumenical dialogue. What about this hypothesis? Has it produced some practical steps, or has it remained on paper?

These questions touch the main object, indeed, of the dialogue between the Catholic Church, and the Orthodox Churches on the other side. There is also an international mixed Catholic-Orthodox commission, with representatives of the fourteen Orthodox Churches. During our meetings, we put on the table this issue, from a long time ago, as the main object of our confrontation, the relationship between primacy and synodality. All the Catholic-Orthodox relations turn on this fulcrum, really. To discuss it is not easy, since we do not want a low-level compromise; we want to put in dialogue the two strengths we are equipped with: synodality, the Orthodox strength, and primacy, the Catholic strength. Then we should rediscover the role the Successor of Peter must play, in the unity of Eastern and Western Churches. It is not an easy work, but I must add, that deepening this question would be useful also in the dialogue with Protestantism.

Pope Francis has held two synods in a short period of time. He has also explicitly said that the Catholic Church needs a *higher* degree of synodality. According to you, could this attitude foster the dialogue with the churches where synodality is more developed?

The core of the ecumenism is the so-called 'gifts exchange', since each Church has a special gift to offer. In the Apostolic Exhortation *Evangelii Gaudium*, Pope Francis mentions this 'gifts exchange' where he says that 'we [Catholics] can learn many things from the Orthodox

Churches, referring to synodality. Primacy and synodality are the two sides of the same coin, as I consider them. We need to deepen the practice of the primacy in the context of the synodality. I am convinced that the Catholic Church has not developed yet the synodality degree potentially practicable as Catholic Church. Along this way yes, we can learn the synodality from other Churches.

You served for a long time as President of the Pontifical Council for Promoting Christian Unity, also for Benedict XVI. How would you characterize Benedict and Francis's approaches to ecumenism? Are there some differences, and what would they be?

In the first place, I see more continuity between them, without even forgetting that all the popes from the age of the Second Vatican Council up to now, not only Benedict XVI and Francis, had the ecumenism at heart. We have just celebrated the fiftieth anniversary of Paul VI first great encounter with the Archbishop of Canterbury and Anglican Primate Michael Ramsey, the other big step towards the orthodoxy is the reconciliation between Constantinople and Rome sanctioned by the encounter in 1964 in Jerusalem with Patriarch Athenagoras. This was followed in 1965 by the revoking of the mutual excommunication.

Following the commitment of John Paul II, then Benedict XVI and Francis, I see continuity, more than anything else. Especially today, a strong emphasis Francis raises on, 'ecumenism of the blood'. It is dependent on the current situation as persecutions of Christians have never been so violent in history. The Pope always repeats that Christians are persecuted not as Orthodox, Oriental, Lutheran, Protestants, Pentecostals, Catholics, and so on. They are persecuted simply as 'Christians', without any distinction among them. Therefore, the blood doesn't divide, the blood unites! At the time of the early Church, Tertullian said that 'the blood of martyrs is seed of new Christians.' Today we could say that the blood of martyrs, the many martyrs Christians of today, will be tomorrow the seed of the unity of all the body of Christ. Francis makes me glad every time he affirms it forcefully, because personally I am really convinced that the ecumenism of martyrs is the centre of ecumenism.

6 ARCHBISHOP JOSEPH E. KURTZ

ARCHBISHOP OF LOUISVILLE & PRESIDENT OF THE UNITED STATES CONFERENCE OF CATHOLIC BISHOPS FROM 2013 TO 2016

The Art of Accompaniment

I am curious if, by chance, your knowledge of Jorge Bergoglio dates back to before his election to the papacy.

NO. I NEVER MET Cardinal Bergoglio. While I had heard of him as a holy and engaged person, I had no in-depth knowledge until his election as Pope.

Was there a meeting or encounter between you that left a special memory?

My first meeting with Pope Francis face to face was in October 2013. At this point, he was the Holy Father for just half a year. I was serving as Vice President and was accompanying Cardinal Timothy Dolan, who was then President of the USCCB, on our annual Curial visits. These curial visits often are concluded with an audience with the Holy Father. I was amazed at our first meeting by his personal and relaxed manner. I recall that he told me that he liked my smile. We met for about 50 minutes and I left very impressed by what I would discover to be one of his hallmarks, seeing the person first!

The opportunity to meet the Pope and talk face to face is reserved for very few people. How is Pope Francis

when one speaks to him in more private situations, away from the television cameras?

Let me repeat the observation I made in response to the previous question. Pope Francis sees the person first. He is also a great conversationalist. When in his presence, there is a healthy and free exchange. He listens, asks questions, and responds well. His manner of dialogue put me at ease very quickly. I can say that I enjoyed that first meeting immensely.

Francis himself tells sometimes, as a joke, that in the Vatican he is considered undisciplined, in the sense that he does not wish to follow some of the pope's previous customs. At the same time, he is able to devote attention to everyone he meets, even simple and humble people. This ability, in your opinion, where does it come from and what does it reveal about the spirit of the Pope?

I see Pope Francis as a pastor of souls, never wanting formality or protocol to get in the way. One of my first impressions was that he is the kind of approachable pastor that I like. I believe that he does not favour a protocol that distances. Where does it come from? I would like to have been a fly on the wall in his home while he was growing up. I would suspect that the human quality was likely all around his home. This is why family is so important to him. I also add that he is truly himself and comfortable with himself. There is not the slightest sense that he is pretending to be anyone other than himself. He is first and foremost interested in the one in front of him.

In the last 50 or 60 years, the figure of the Pope has changed enormously, especially in the way people imagine the role, and Pope Francis is contributing a

lot to this change. Some observers have spoken controversially of 'desacralisation' of the figure of the Pope. How would you respond to this criticism?

I see Pope Francis's contribution to the figure of the Pope as positive. Since I was in high school, I have experienced six popes but only the last three I met in person. I must say that I have seen the humanity of each and have seen each as pastor in a unique way. They seem to be summed well by Cardinal Jean-Louis Pierre Tauran, I believe, when he said that the faithful came to the Vatican to see Pope St John Paul II, listen to Benedict XVI and to touch Francis. I believe there is truth to the continuity of pastoral presences. The perspective of looking back in 2050 would help, but I can already say that Pope Francis has captured the popular imagination as a caring, accessible spiritual leader. I believe what has added to this is his practice of simple, engaging morning homilies and his interviews. I am not the only one who checks out his homilies for my morning use in the USA time zone! His genre is original, and we as a Church welcome this gift well. The tone and content of a homily is not the same genre as an encyclical. Even his encyclicals seem to include that exhortatory style. In him, I see one who seeks to live as Jesus asks. This approach deepens the figure of the Pope.

To those who comment that the changes of certain customs implemented by Pope Francis are 'desacralisation', what are your thoughts in response this suggestion?

I prefer to see Pope Francis as bringing his pastoral presence and humanity as have the recent popes preceding him. He explains the changes he makes. His lodging allows him more regular contact with a consistent community at Eucharist and meals. His choice of name and car are gestures to the simplicity that he preaches. Each pope brings his gifts and unique personality to this figure of the 'servant of the servants.'

As a minister of service in unity with Christ and His people, Pope Francis also is clear that he preserves faithfully what has been passed on to him. He does so by putting into practice what Pope Benedict has proposed as *ressourcement,* 'a return to the roots.' In this root meaning, Pope Francis is 'radical' in his call to return to Jesus and His commission to preach to all nations.

Pope Francis is a person who has developed a certain degree of 'celebrity status', with all the attention that he is attracting also by people who are not Catholic and those who in the past may not have been interested in the Church. Based on his experience as a bishop, in contact with people, what would you say is the trait or traits of Francis that most impress people?

Most see first his turning from stiff formality and seeing the person first, especially the forgotten person. This is what endears him. A closer look reveals his radical return to Jesus, foreshadowed in Benedict's engaging three volumes *Jesus of Nazareth,* calling us to encounter Jesus and His call to go forth. He is the antidote to a 'turned-in-on-itself' culture. People sense that he understands their loneliness. These actions contribute to his popularity and celebrity.

Much has been spoken regarding his simplicity and sobriety. We think of the cars, such as the very basic Ford Focus model and, choosing his residence at the guesthouse Santa Marta. Francis goes to great lengths to avoid being identified as a man of power, like the Popes of the past surrounded by their, one could say, 'royal court'. The world has met with favour the message he has launched, but sometimes it seems to

have brought some confusion in the Church. Is that the case?

His way of communicating through morning homilies and informal interviews is a genre that was at first relatively new to us. I believe that he is aware of this and thus in *Amoris Laetitia*, he urges that his message be read slowly and patiently. I believe that he expects to challenge in a positive way with his words. He also engages in dialogue, witnessed in the synod process.

The press welcomed with much fanfare Pope Francis's many gestures and words, which seemed surprising and new, given some are new, and some just seem it. What is the occasion in which you personally were the most surprised by Francis?

I watched him rest on the airplane between Washington DC and New York City. My seat on the plane was behind and to the right of him. It was my first time seeing him not busy pastorally but at rest. He prayed privately, ate a little and then rested. I could not help but think that he must be exhausted. Then, once the crowd was seen when we touched down at NYC, he was renewed. He has said that the gift of great energy has been given to him as Pope. I saw this first hand and marvelled.

Another aspect of Pope Francis which has warranted much attention has been his, more or less, strong and explicit complaints or criticism against the Roman Curia. Sometimes, it seemed that his opinion was not positive. Moreover, he was elected Pope after a period marked by several scandals. What do you think of all this?

Many have noted that at the time of the papal election a major theme of conversations was the call for renewal of the Curia. In an increasingly global church, a mindset of service is required, a service that listens. I see this in the archdiocesan staff with whom I serve. We are called to be renewed in service to the faithful in parishes. I believe that Pope Francis has taken this call for renewal of the Curia seriously. This is seen in the efforts concerning the economic structures as well as a call to be responsive to the pastoral needs on the ground.

The word mercy is the word one could say sums up the meaning of Pope Francis's pontificate. In your opinion, why is Pope Francis so sensitive to this theme?

His call for mercy is not abstract. He called himself a sinner when first asked and recalls the experience of confession as a late teen. I believe that he has meditated on Jesus in his mercy to him and has taken the parables seriously. He is a man of great compassion who wants to do to others as he would like them to do to him.

Pope Francis recalls often, throughout his priesthood, how he confessed penitents on various occasions and why this is necessary for him. Why is this experience so important for a priest?

Next to experiencing forgiveness personally, the need to have an ear to the real plight of people is essential to the Servant of Jesus. In the confessional, a trust in God's forgiving presence breaks down barriers and so we see the person in her need more clearly than anywhere else. Hearing confessions grounds the priest in pastoral charity.

Often, Francis offers confessors much advice. Is there one piece of advice in particular that you try to put into practice?

When someone enters the confessional, I ask Jesus to help me see them as the only one who will be confessing to me today. There is something refreshing about welcoming someone in a unique way and it brings out tender care in my soul.

For the press, Pope Francis is a very popular character. In fact, much of the press internationally devote a great deal of attention to him. In your opinion, 'the Francis' that the press reports, is that the real Francis, the authentic one? Is there something that remains not said by media, therefore remaining in the shadows that is not seen or heard?

I believe that Pope Francis presents himself privately and publicly in a consistent way. By and large, the media have conveyed him well. Of course, the news cycle is such that often there is a tendency to give quotes in isolation and it is necessary for all to give Pope Francis room to proclaim his full message. Some accounts of media might focus only on what is a perspective that they are seeking to promote. Likewise, we the readers might look only at the soundbite or headline. With Pope Francis, there is always more.

Some people say that Pope Francis is liked too much, by too many people. In this way, some try to suggest that he is not raising controversial issues, in order to avoid criticism. Perhaps even to the extent that they suggest he avoids that which could make some not like him. Have you ever happened to hear such a remark? What do you think about it?

I think that Pope Francis is consistent with what he calls all to do, keep eyes on the gaze of Jesus and point to Jesus rather than to himself. I do not believe that Pope Francis seeks to avoid the challenging directions of Jesus reflected in Church teachings. This is evident in the reading of his encyclicals and exhortations in their entirety.

His warnings against financial speculation, the globalization of indifference, the throwaway culture, the exploitation of the planet, have also resulted in some arguing Francis is an anti-capitalist Pope. What do you think about this accusation? Are there grounds for it?

I believe that Pope Francis's strong call is consistent with Pope St John Paul II's appeals for a stronger commitment for the common good. Like John Paul II, he calls for conversion, especially from those with influence to have an effect on those downtrodden in the world. His experience of South America, as John Paul's of Poland, has made his words very vivid, especially as he speaks of global indifference and a throwaway culture.

Yet, Francis's teaching on the themes of the family, of marriage, and defence of life does not have the same impact. Why is that, in your opinion?

Pope Francis has called two synods early on and both have been on renewal of the family. In his call for concern about care of Creation, in his encyclical *Laudato Si*, he presents what he calls an integral ecology that seeks human dignity and the common good for Creation. It is the case that media reports will tend to emphasize what is the priority of their organization. It is important that we give room for the full message of Pope Francis and that we as a Church, use these occasions for local renewal to ensure that full impact.

After two Synods on the Family, what has concretely changed? Regarding *Amoris Laetitia*, there are many

different interpretations. In your opinion, where is the novelty, if there is one?

It is early to judge. Looking back at St John Paul II's *Pastores Dabo Vobis* of 1992, I can see the renewal of seminary formation that flowed from this exhortation. These fruits may not have been evident in the first year of its publication. Likewise, these next years are critical in the receiving and implementing of the vision of *Amoris Laetitia* as we renew family life, raise up modern witnesses to the priority of the family and seek to accompany those who struggle. The exhortation contains the advice of Pope Francis to receive the vision slowly and patiently. On the other hand, I have seen already the immediate effect of *Mitis Iudex* with the streamlining of the process of annulments. Without changing teachings, the procedural changes have had an effect in our Archdiocesan Tribunal of more prompt pastoral decisions and more couples turning to the Church for aid in their pastoral circumstances.

Another issue on which Francis said strong words and made significant gestures is the theme of immigration in the world today. His repeated invitation is to build bridges, not walls. In your opinion, how far can you reach solidarity with migrants, without the reception becoming unmanageable for a given nation, or for society?

Pope Francis's pastoral leadership in seeing each immigrant as a person with dignity is having good effect. While he is not proposing a blueprint for a nation's immigration policy, he is forcefully bringing the plight to the world's attention. The USCCB has been forthright in advocating for just immigration reform that is humane and respects sovereign rights of nations. The Church has also taken the lead in reaching out to immigrant families to address both the needs and the gifts of recently arrived families. I believe that Pope Francis's leadership will have a good effect on our efforts for just treatment of all immigrant families.

The theme of migration is linked to that of poverty. Francis always repeats that the essence of Christianity are the works of corporal mercy. He has made many significant gestures of solidarity by setting an example in the Vatican, in Rome and in his travels throughout Italy and around the world. Can it be said that, in this way, he has returned a bit of 'concreteness' to the Christian concept of human dignity?

Pope Francis as a true pastor of souls does not remain abstract but touches the real lives of people, in his words, his gestures and his life of ministry for Christ. This is very true in his reaching out in mercy especially to those who migrate for a better life or seek refuge from political harm. The Church at her best has always sought to welcome the stranger as Jesus has commanded.

Religions in this beginning of the Third Millennium have again become a very important factor in international politics, the cultural debate, and many social phenomena. Religions have become causes of conflict and division between people and cultures. Is it possible to establish a dialogue between very different religions and cultures? Pope Francis, in this respect, expresses a very open, very confident approach. Is it a realistic attitude or not?

Pope Francis consistently calls all to go out to the other and receive others with deep human respect. This is especially true when there are deep values that divide. Rather than ignore these differences, Pope Francis calls us to move from debate to dialogue and never to give up on the power of

God's grace to move hearts. Such dialogue is impelled by a deep desire for a unity in truth and charity for which Jesus prayed on the night before He died, and by a deep respect for every human being. While such a path is complex, Pope Francis rightly believes it is the only true path.

The trip to the United States was long, full of encounters, and meaningful words. What did he leave the Church in the United States?

It is surely too early to give the final word on the fruits of Pope Francis's 2015 journey to the United States. Papal visits continue to give gifts for generations. His public civic events at the White House, Congress, Independence Hall, the United Nations and Ground Zero all produced strong messages that focused on the common good. These themes left a good foundation for continued action in the priorities of the Bishops' Conference, most especially in the efforts for a call to service, a common-sense support for religious freedom and a 'walking with' those most vulnerable in our society. His encouraging words to the United States Bishops in Washington and his deeply pastoral and intimate words to families in Philadelphia will leave, I believe, a lasting legacy for pastoral life and prepared well for the Apostolic Exhortation *Amoris Laetitia*. I also believe that Pope Francis returned to the Vatican with a very uplifting impression of the Church in the States and of the people as very generous, warm and faith filled.

The press and public opinion consider Pope Ratzinger and Pope Bergoglio to be two very different personalities. In this undeniable diversity, in your opinion, is there something that unites them?

While it is true that the personalities and gifts of Pope Emeritus Benedict and Pope Francis are unique, I see so many points of continuity. Pope Francis's highlighting of the proclamation of Jesus and his *ressourcement* 'return to the sources,' find strong foundations in Pope Benedict. This is especially seen in the three-volume Jesus of Nazareth, published by Pope Benedict, not as an encyclical but as a modern, accessible commentary on Jesus, our Saviour. Using very distinct personal traits and gifts, each Pope points to Jesus and to the need for conversion to Him and service to others through His power.

Francis has repeatedly said to regard his predecessor's resignation as an 'open door.' Can the papacy become an 'office' or a fixed-term service?

I understand that most recently Pope Francis has indicated no plans to consider the path which Pope Benedict took at the age of almost 86, being the fourth oldest Pope in history! While not holding simply a secular office but rather an office of service directed by the Holy Spirit, Pope Francis will continue to discern the best path for his service to Christ and the faithful. It is premature to see a pattern.

Pope Francis is the first pope from the Americas in history. All statistical surveys say that Europe is no longer the centre of gravity of world Catholicism. Can we say that Pope Francis, being an American pope, has opened a door?

It would be best to refer to the cardinal electors who elected Pope Francis, a bishop from South America, as opening a door. I had the privilege of serving as a delegate to the Synod on Evangelization in October 2012. Clearly evident at that synod in the composition of delegates and discussion was the global nature of the Catholic Church. It was instructive that during the proceedings of that Synod, Pope Benedict created six new cardinals, representing virtually every continent. Pope Francis has continued this direction to acknowledge the diversity within the Catholic Church by creating cardinals of great diversity, who will be charged with future elections. I believe that this opens the door that views the Church from a perspective beyond Europe.

7 Father Federico Lombardi, SJ

Director of the Holy See Press Office from 2006 to 2016

The Lord Has Granted the Pope a Particular Gift

Fr Lombardi, I would like to ask you when you first met Jorge Bergoglio.

PERHAPS IT WOULD surprise people, but before the pontificate, I did not know Bergoglio well. Our only encounter happened at the General Congregation of Jesuits in 1983, that which elected Provost General of the Jesuits Father Peter-Hans Kolvenbach. I was participating representing Italian Jesuits, and he for the Argentinians. There were more than 200 of us priests present and there was no particular way to get to know each other. In any case, I certainly knew who he was and what he was doing as auxiliary bishop, then archbishop, cardinal. During the congregation meetings before the conclave, there was a brief greeting along the corridor. Honestly no, there was not a profound way of knowing each other.

Then, the election happened. The first encounter was the day after, at Santa Maria Maggiore where he would go to pray before Mary *Salus Populi Romani,* 'Protectress of the Roman People'. I was part of the restricted group accompanying him and at the end, the Pope greeted everyone personally including myself. I remember observing well the spontaneity of the atmosphere and the intensity of prayer. It is lovely to think back to it, that my first encounter with him happened there where Pope Francis would return so many times to pray in the most important moments.

Pope Francis is a very active Pope, 'very present' on mass media. Does he 'tire you out' more than other popes?

Certainly, one must always learn what is the situation in which one finds himself. As I have always said, changing the pontificate also changes the style of the pope. It is not so much the 'service' given by who collaborates with him in communications that changes, but the way of serving.

Tiring? Well, honestly, I believe I have always worked intensely. I had three assignments between Vatican Radio, the Vatican Television Centre and the Holy See Press Office. There was little time to rest. I would not know how to say if and when I worked more or less, because they are different situations. At times, one works so much with tension and worry, and at times, it is all simpler, but there is still much to do. We could say that there were moments with Benedict XVI that I too with my work, had to confront situations of suffering, which we know well: the sexual abuse crisis that was very painful, the leak of reserved documents, or tensions and discussions inside the Curia, of which the press often speaks. In these delicate, painful cases it is necessary to find the most objective and reassuring possible interpretation.

During the pontificate of Francis, the prolonged periods of worry were less. If anything, there was the issue of the Pope's 'dynamism'. Let's take the two synods which I experienced in the Press Office with so many things to do. In particular with the second, we found a way very different from the prior synods: Before there were bulletins upon bulletins, written interventions, during that time instead we did more personal communications with briefings each day with guests and personal witnesses who spoke with journalists.

However, there is always so much work, at times attributed to an event's intensity or at times, having to do with the amount of suffering of a question like the first Vatileaks or the scandals.

Does Francis ever make specific requests regarding the press or mass media? Obviously, I refer to talks that were not strictly confidential.

In general, he will enlist my opinion about requests he receives for interviews, messages and so on. This is normally one of the services he asks of me. It is done very freely, sometimes deciding without any need for me and that is great, too. It is obvious that these items may come to the Director of the Holy See Press Office. Overall, I must say that he is very spontaneous. He has the gift of the capacity to understand what, when, how to communicate; in that case, the opinion of the director is marginal.

Francis is the Pope that has been the most involved in reforming Vatican communications. I imagine you spoke about this. What does Pope Francis desire from this reform?

To tell the truth, I was not very involved with these particular responsibilities. However, having worked in this field for over 25 years, I had foreseen both the situations and problems.

It seemed absolutely clear to me that for many years that which needed to be reviewed were the communications systems of the Holy See. It has a long and beautiful history, composed of many types of media, each a bit 'separate' from one another: the typography, *L'Osservatore Romano*, radio, television, internet site and so on. I speak of all the types of media born from the evolution of communication technology, which respond to the same mission, but are autonomous with regard to management and administration.

Now instead, the evolution of technology produces an 'interweaving' convergence of media. That is indeed the process I lived, for example, as Director of Vatican Radio. It was not a radio any longer, in the strict sense of the word, since we used to publish texts on the Internet, along with photos and videoclips. It became a 'multimedia' reality, as occurred in other Vatican media. Therefore, it had become completely clear how urgent it was to reorganise together the whole system, to take in hand the issue and to courageously face it.

The context changes, but not the mission which always remains the same, namely to announce the Gospel of Jesus Christ serving the Catholic Church for the humanity of today, and understanding the problems, situations, and diversity among people and nations. What is changing are the ways, wording, historical contexts, and therefore the technology and ways of expression. Best wishes to those who will do this tomorrow and beyond. I did what I could do.

Pope Francis has often appeared on the first page of newspapers with gestures or declarations which are very surprising. Was there an occasion when you were surprised the most?

My greatest surprise was his election, the election of a Jesuit Pope. I did not expect it. I did not have any candidates in mind, or preferences. That is to say, for me, a Jesuit like him, it is not spontaneous to think a Jesuit who lives a life of service could become pope, or bishop or cardinal. Therefore, it was rather surprising to me for there to be a Jesuit Pope. It was totally unexpected. Naturally, if this is the will of God, if the Holy Spirit brings us in this direction, if the cardinals decided this, I accept it very willingly [he laughs]. The common spirituality of the Society of Jesus, the Ignatius spirituality creates a certain naturalness in comprehending a series of attitudes, perspectives, and spiritual sensibilities maybe less familiar to others.

Discernment is a theme so characteristic of this pontificate. To find the will of God, without thinking that everything is written and clear in black and white, is the journey. This style is very simple and close to the people. Concentrating on the figure of Jesus, the Gospel, is a very concrete way to relate to everyday life, as one sees in the Pope's morning homilies at his residence Casa Santa Marta. They are all things I find very familiar and not surprising. I do not ask myself where it comes from, because to me I seem to understand very well from our spirituality and common formation.

Therefore, in a way it was a surprise, but in another, the advantage of a certain spiritual tuning. In reading the history and journey of the Church, you find that everything is a journey and you continually must seek the will of God. The will of God is always in front of you. You need to discover it through signs, because God works in the way around you, you must recognise it and understand where he calls you. This sense of surprise that God always surprises you, has something new to tell you and it is not something you can control or take in your hands.

Certainly, Francis is a Pope who brings about much curiosity and much attention, also in lay and secular press, even the press of non-Catholic countries. In all this talk about what Francis does, do you find the true authentic Francis and the true sense of his teaching? How is Pope Francis, as a person, away from the cameras?

I have a certain trust that the people and the media understand certain fundamental aspects of the message of Francis. His message that he speaks and repeats in every way is that God wants the good for His creatures and good for His people. There is a message of mercy. The mercy expresses the heart of God. God is always ready to pardon and is welcoming. God does not exclude anyone. It is man that excludes on his own, but the Lord goes always to search to embrace man again.

These fundamental messages to me seem to be welcomed pretty well in general by the people and by the media. What the people understand is not very different than what many media, in their much more popular aspect, understand. Moreover, the media are many things, not just articles, images, through which the people understand Francis well. They appreciate his expressions of tenderness manifested with concrete gestures, closeness and the love of God. If there was not the media, no one would have seen nor heard. We live in a world where we cannot do without mass media.

The authority of Francis, his charm at an international level beyond the differences of culture is not something superficial. He is not the 'star' that strikes curiosity or imagination. It is the charm of a spiritual leader. We could say 'substantial' on many themes, such as attention for the poor, the concern for humanity today in the ecological sphere, the imbalances among people, the unjust conflicts, the world war in pieces, the human trafficking.

The people understand that Pope Francis is a leader that is concerned with the true and large questions for humanity today, with a spirit of love and attention especially for the poor and the suffering. The media can then make their mistakes: to be superficial, conflict the issues, solicit stupid curiosities like always! Overall, in their specific case, they help the people understand Francis.

Therefore, I am rather optimistic. At the start of the pontificate, the media and its operators were at their time helped by Francis. Francis helped the media by his charisma to communicate in such simple and effective ways, to rediscover positive aspects of their task and their vocation. As I have said previously, during the best times of Pope St John Paul II's pontificate, the communicators are normal, good or bad people, like everyone with their defects. Perhaps at times they are at the service of certain interests or need to obey their publications, but they are happy if they can tell something positive. One would be perverse to enjoy recounting only the negative, ugly stories. In the end, they basically are very happy if they can tell there is peace and not more war. It is good if people manage to have dialogue, rather than pulling out each other's hair.

We could say that the effectiveness of Francis and the ease of understanding his message helped many communicators to find the joy of being able to say positive things. Many of them became his allies, because of his joy. Communication also has many defects, superficiality, researching scandal, seeing the negative rather than the positive, plotting who is with the Pope and who is against, what seems to be a great idiocy. Still with their defects and mistakes, the media collaborated and collaborate for the 'positive' for the pontificate of Francis.

What is the greatest misunderstanding about Francis, if you believe there is one?

There are not many misunderstandings about Francis. It depends if one's attitude is closed-minded and is unable to understand the mission of Francis, the Church, and Vatican ecclesiastically. A misunderstanding occurs when one reads all of a reality and we could say 'political' terms or relationship of forces but without the capacity to see a more profound dynamic.

You could read the Synod of Bishops as a furious struggle between who wanted a rigid affirmation of doctrine and another who wanted that everyone does as he or she believe. Therefore, they fight, but this is not the reality! The reality is the people have good intentions and try to understand the Gospel or tradition of the Church. This dynamic is not always easy because it requires respect, listening, and then seeking together the journey.

The problem is to understand or not understand the reality of the Church and who Francis is and what he does in the Church, as a spiritual guide for everyone.

Is it the case of those who say that today there is not only one Pope?

These are only silly thoughts. There is a Pope, Francis. The Pope Emeritus chose to dedicate himself to prayer and not exercising the ministry of guiding the Church. During the interview on the flight from Armenia to Rome, Pope Francis said this clearly.

Some speak of a 'censored' Francis in the media when faced with sensitive themes against the Church's Teachings, such as abortion, contraception, gay marriage, euthanasia, and gender manipulation. Do you ever have this impression yourself?

This is always a temptation of the media and communicators, which is also pretty understandable. One sees that for them all goes well while the other seeks instead to not discuss it to make it pass under silence. It is nothing new it is something that always happens, but not only to Francis. It happens in all areas not just those of the Church or of morals. Certainly, there are interpretations in some ways 'partial' for wanting to sustain a certain position, but I would not be surprised or say that they touch only Francis. I believe it also happened with Benedict XVI and John Paul II, with everyone!

Nevertheless, what could happen with Francis is that his great authority and popularity makes it more difficult to criticize him, since everyone could think to themselves, 'Well, this is such an immense authority that if I start to speak poorly about him, I could lose more than him.' In other cases, instead, to criticize is much easier and one gathers others who think like him too. Maybe someone notes that with Francis, since he enjoys great respect from the people, one has more fear of emphasizing positions that are different than his. Since his authority is so great, he does not have the courage to say anything contrary. This could have its truth. However, it is true too that to tell the things in a more favourable light for oneself is always common. It was not invented yesterday or today, it has always been that way.

One says often that Francis is a Pope that speaks above all with gestures. To offer an example, I think of when he was just elected and decided to celebrate the Washing of the Feet in a juvenile detention centre. Could we say that it is his speaking with gestures that explains a bit his popularity?

We could say that this type of gesture, completed with this way of doing so, was not 'invented' with the pontificate. They are consistent with what he used to do as Archbishop of Buenos Aires. Then becoming Pope, they seemed new and were treated with particular emphasis.

The effectiveness of many gestures touches the hearts and minds of many people. He understands people well.

This is a gift he possesses, a kindness that is expressed with a natural, spontaneity from the heart which is evident when he approaches, the children, the elderly, and the sick. Certainly, Francis is aware of their expressiveness, but they come from his heart. They correspond very well to an ancient pedagogy of the Church.

The Washing of the Feet for instance, he did not invent! The Washing of the Feet comes from Jesus, correct? and similarly other gestures. For example, the Fridays of Mercy during the Jubilee Year of Mercy, gestures that he compels us also to do. These gestures were in the tradition of the Church from the beginning, from the Gospel of Matthew 25. He certainly did not invent them. However, it is necessary to say that he helps us rediscover these gestures in a very concrete and effective way.

However, there were also small incidents regarding the Pope and mass media, one of them being on the return flight from Manila on how many children should Catholics have, or the 'punch' to Mr Alberto Gasbarri, the former organizer of the papal trips. 'He is a good friend, but if he says a swear word against my mother, then a punch awaits him', was the example made by Francis on the limits of the freedom of speech. Certainly, the immediacy and spontaneity are very appreciated by journalists but they also bring about some risks. What do you think?

In the way Pope Francis handles these very spontaneous conversations, it would be a miracle if there were never a word that provoked some problem, an unfavourable response, or could be misinterpreted in an imprecise manner. At the same time, the journalists and intelligent people are aware that this way of expressing oneself needs to be understood with the appropriate hermeneutics. It is not calculated, but it is a spontaneous way of expressing oneself. If I study everything in advance, up until the last comma, then I cannot be spontaneous anymore.

Therefore, we have this spontaneous, rich, abundant way of expressing oneself, if you like a dialogue in which you ask and the Pope listens and responds there, in the moment, refining his thoughts little by little. You either want this or you do not want this! If you want the perfect, doctrinal, ready to transcribe in a book answer, then you cannot have the spontaneity.

Although inconvenient, spontaneous and sincere communication needs to be interpreted with benevolence for its true meaning. Intelligent people understand this. If one has a poor disposition from the beginning and tries always to find fault, that person, in my opinion, demonstrates that he does not understand the 'positive' of what the Pope does.

If, however, everyone is tired after days and days of travel and the journalists ask questions that the Pope is not prepared to respond to, perhaps an interview is not always a good idea.

Everything can be done better. Everything has its limits. The conversation with the journalists travelling together with the pope is a nice tradition, started with blessed Paul VI and developed especially with Pope St John Paul II. It has always been appreciated by the journalists, as a good way for carrying ahead a relationship between the pope and the operators of the media. Without a doubt, it could still be improved, paying attention to the personality of the pope and the particular situation in which it happens. Francis with his very long conversations on the flights is very characteristic of his way of being. Moreover, even during interviews aside from the planes, I saw various times that the style is always a relaxed conversation, very spontaneous, without prepared formulas beforehand but with a flow. His style of dialogue is a searching for the response in the same moment without formula, but rather a sense of presence and participation with he who poses the question.

At times, it is ok. At times he has told me that he was rather disappointed by the questions received. He did not find them very interesting. After a lovely and interesting trip, he was perhaps hoping for questions on the experience. Instead journalists usually think, 'Well, ok, about the visit we have already spoken, now let us take the occasion to ask something else,' anything else that enters the mind. Therefore, a consideration one could also make in the way journalists can use the opportunity given to them, is to say if they use it well or not.

In any case, Francis has always demonstrated continuing to enjoy these interviews, because no one requires him to spend an hour each time. I ask always, 'How much time do you want to dedicate this time?' and he responds, 'an hour', always given that it is not too short a flight. For him, it is a service to the community of communicators, an availability that he wishes to offer to those present on the flight, and through them, of course, to all communicators in general. I find it to be a very lovely thing. If then something happens inconvenient, then, with the good will of everyone and the intelligence of those present, perhaps something could still be clarified. The interview on the flight remains in any case, with Francis, a beautiful witness of the spirit with which the Pope moves in relation to the people, the Church. He communicates with sincerity, spontaneity, transparency, tranquillity and trust. It does not seem to me to be the case to sacrifice this practice because every so often a word is not understood. It would be absolutely disproportionate.

We remember also that Francis, conversing with journalists on the papal flight, made a biblical reference to Daniel in the lion's den. Perhaps by chance is there something behind the scenes, behind this joke?

No. However, I would make another reflection. For those who used to know Bergoglio in Argentina this familiarity in conversing with journalists especially on papal flights is something new in his life, because in Argentina he used to have a lot of prudence and many reluctances with journalists and interviews. Many that knew him previously, now are a bit surprised that he has established this very spontaneous and positive relationship with journalists be it during the flights, or with the interviews he has granted. It means that if ever he felt like Daniel among the lions, namely the journalists, he felt completely supported by the grace of God. Not only was he not torn to pieces, but moreover the lions were at ease with him.

Many in Argentina now note in his a vitality that connects to 'the grace of the state'. It means the particular help that today the Lord gives to him to perform His service, that can be observed in Francis's energy, capacity, inspiration; the possibility that he never could have imagined to have, even from a physical point of view. The spontaneity and the ease of this good relationship with the media forms a part of this particular grace that the Lord has given him.

Pope Francis is very much launched in the world of social media, but this presence is also a bit controversial at least for some. Do you think it is still a choice for a Pope to have a social profile or has it become a necessity?

I am convinced that it is not Francis who says, 'Let's do a Tweet, now let's do Instagram, now let's do YouTube', and who knows what else tomorrow. Francis does what he must do. He does 'the Pope', with the typical spontaneity of his way of being. People in charge of communicating who is Pope Francis and what he does, they simply capture his signals and relaunch them in the world of media. Then, we could say, Francis is particularly made for some social media. He offers to them a particularly adapted material. For example, concrete and effective brief phrases are ideal for a tweet, like certain facial expressions or gestures like embracing the sick are ideal for Instagram. No?

There could be another pope that perhaps would not be ideal for Instagram. He will be ideal instead for writing a serious, and systematic volume of catechesis on certain themes, maybe. Every pope will have his way of communicating. Francis is perfectly 'in tune' with the social media communication. Today the social media are very effective and pervasive because they transmit profound contents through a few words or a simple image. Francis is certainly more 'in tune' with them than Benedict XVI, but it does not mean that Benedict's way of communication is not valuable, particularly his clearness, completeness, and absolutely extraordinary capacity to synthesize.

I remember that it was Benedict XVI who started to use Twitter, and YouTube too. I remember when we proposed to him the small videoclips together with Monsignor Claudio Maria Celli, who was president of the Pontifical Council for Social Communications, who said, 'It will create clamour, to announce that the Pope has a channel on YouTube.' In fact, the Vatican Press Office was really crowded, when we presented the initiative. If in five or six years there emerges a new social media, we will see if it will be adapted to the Pope.

Is there anything you would still like to add about Pope Francis?

I would say that Francis is a man that knows how to gather the global questions of humanity today, see the encyclical *Laudato Si* on the safeguarding of Creation. He has become an authority on a worldwide level, capable of giving authoritative responses, especially to questions related to the ecological crisis.

With regard to his coming from Latin America, this fact has undoubtedly generated an enhanced sensibility of the Universal Church for the great problems of humanity. Themes like attention for the poor, or the battle against marginalization are yes, valid for all, but also are an inheritance of something that in the Latin American Church is very alive. Now we feel enriched by this perspective, like we did with the Polish Pope St John Paul II and his experiences confronting totalitarianism. Each pope brings to the See of Peter his own specific richness that becomes enrichment for the whole Church.

8 CARDINAL GERHARD LUDWIG MULLER

PREFECT EMERITUS OF THE CONGREGATION FOR THE DOCTRINE OF THE FAITH

The Charisma of Francis that Opens Even the Most Closed Hearts

When was your first encounter with Jorge Mario Bergoglio? Do you have a particular memory of that encounter?

The first time was during the 2001 Synod consecrated to the theme, 'The Bishop Servant of the Gospel of Jesus Christ for the Hope of the World.' I was participating as an expert. It was during the work of the synod that there was the attack on the Twin Towers in New York. Cardinal Egan, Archbishop of New York, was Relator at the Synod and had to return immediately to his city. Pope St John Paul II replaced him with the Cardinal of Buenos Aires. We, members of the College of Experts, were led by Cardinal Bergoglio, from that point forward as the point of reference for the work. In those days, I could speak with him in Spanish. Before that time, I had been at least 15 times in Latin America, whether for theological encounters in various universities, or for missionary, pastoral experiences. Twelve years later, Pope Francis granted me my first audience with him as Pontiff and I was Prefect of the Congregation for the Doctrine of the Faith.

What importance does it have for the Universal Church to have a Pope from Latin America?

What is important for the Church is the closeness to Jesus Christ who is her leader everywhere in the world. Given that, all the Churches with their bishop are united in concrete communion to the Successor of Peter, who is always the Bishop of Rome. Peter and Paul, the Princes of the Apostles, witnessed Jesus Christ in Rome not only with word, but with their blood. From the beginning, the Bishops of Rome were not just Romans or Italians. Throughout the centuries, especially in the First of Christian history, there were also popes from Greece, Syria, and other places of the Roman Empire; subsequently from France, Germany, and more recently from Poland. In our times, marked by globalization, it is easier to expand the radius from where one can come.

The word mercy has become the key word in the pontificate of Pope Francis. In your opinion, from where does this sensibility come?

Mercy expresses the central reason of the universal saving will of God. Nowadays, many people do not know anymore how to place themselves in front of sin, in front of man's fragility. Instead of letting us be judged by God, people close in on themselves, in their fault, trying to resolve the problem, in order to survive, denying it. The solution however is entrusting oneself to God fully and completely. Mercy is for God not only a generic attitude of benevolence towards us. God brought it to fruition with death of His Son on the Cross. 'For God so loved the world that He gave His Only Son, so that everyone who believes in Him might not perish but have eternal life' (Jn 3:16). The entire Church can and should be grateful for Pope Francis emphasizing the closeness of God and the mercy that perfects us, does not oppress us.

Pope Francis enjoys a great popularity with the press. He is respected, listened to, and some would say exalted. In your opinion is 'the Francis' of the press and TV the true, authentic Francis?

I rejoice that Pope Francis is recognized by much of the mass media that were traditionally critical towards the Pope and the Catholic Church. Francis has a charisma that enables him to open even the most closed hearts. The lovingness of the Pope is almost the holy door of the love of God. A door offered to everyone to encounter Christ.

The press has welcomed with much attention the various gestures and words of the Pope, that could seem surprising and new. What is the occasion in which you personally felt the most surprised and moved by Francis?

When the Pope turns with great affection to the most suffering, especially those afflicted with severe facial deformities from illness, this is what impressed me the most. It is easy to preach love towards your neighbour, however, difficult to put it into practice. Managing to get over the disgust, that is simply a natural reaction, again is what impressed me the most.

You have a vast, very meaningful experience behind you, as you tell in your book *On the Side of the Poor: The Theology of Liberation*, published by LEV in 2014. I refer to the periods of study and pastoral service you spent in Peru, in the slums of Lima and among the farmers of the Andes. What has remained with you from that experience?

That experience has expanded my horizon. I saw the universality of the Church. In theory, we all know the universality of God for all men; however, for a German like me, it would be much easier to move to a European country with a culture similar to Germany. In Latin America, I directly 'experimented' with what poverty really is, the poverty of the misery of man, often without being able to satisfy their fundamental primary needs. Millions of people live below levels of human dignity, the dignity that does not disappear even in the poorest of the poor, since every man is made in the image and likeness of God. The Holy Father has repeated various times that the Church is concerned not only in the material progress of man. We must announce the Gospel to the poor too, so that the Word of the Love of God arrives to them. We feel ourselves responsible of an integral development of the human person and of society.

That continent until today had never given a Pope to the Catholic Church, although it is the one most populated with Catholic people. In your opinion, will this novelty produce permanent changes for the future?

Francis's pontificate has opened a new horizon, has brought in governing the Church the culture of a deeply Catholic continent like Latin America. The mission and the task of the Pope are always the same. The men called to be Successor of Peter are concrete men, each one with his own story that gives his personal touch to the Petrine Ministry. This fact contributes to the richness, charisms, and gifts with which the Holy Spirit fills His Church in this precise time of history.

A poor Church for the poor, how should it really be?

The Church needs material means to complete Her mission. Those materials are truly the means, and not the goal of the Mission of the Church. To help the poor, we need material resources, but we also need priests, lay people, religious with a good theological formation and solid personal motivation, which comes from Christ, the Good Shepherd. Therefore, it is necessary to invest energy and resources for a personal formation of this type.

When we speak of a 'Church for the poor', do we speak even of 'moral' poverty? To be honest, today there are a lot of 'poor' people who have lost a sense of morality, due also to our very relativistic and permissive culture in some areas of personal life like family, sexuality and marriage.

Certainly, this is another shade of poverty, the 'moral' poverty. In so many people today, there is a lacking of something essential for human existence, namely to have God as treasure, as sense of life, as orientation for the journey, as joy and hope for existence. The Church exists for this, at the end of the day, in order that the question in the heart of man does not extinguish and the announcement proclaimed by Christ may be welcomed by each of us.

9 CARDINAL WILFRID NAPIER, OFM

ARCHBISHOP OF DURBAN, SOUTH AFRICA

Building the Church with Faith and Works, a Witness to Jesus with His Own Life

I am curious if, by chance, your knowledge of Jorge Bergoglio dates back to before his election to the papacy.

MY KNOWLEDGE OF Cardinal Jorge Bergoglio dates back to 2001 when we were both installed as Cardinals by Pope St John Paul II. Thereafter we did not go much beyond a nodding acquaintance. We met often during consistories. The acquaintance deepened somewhat during the Conclave of 2005 when his name was prominent among the candidates.

Was there a meeting or encounter between you that left a special memory?

The encounter that remains special was when I went up to greet and congratulate him on becoming our new Pope. What made it special was that just prior to our going up to greet him, Pope Francis had walked half the length of the Sistine Chapel to greet Cardinal Ivan Dias, where he was seated. The Pope had taken into account that Cardinal Dias had difficulty walking. That gesture of humility and supreme consideration for others will remain a landmark memory of Pope Francis.

The opportunity to meet the Pope and talk face-to-face is reserved for very few people, but how is Pope Francis when one speaks to him in more private situations, away from the television cameras?

Face-to-face encounters have been many and varied. There is one that stands out as it reveals much about Pope Francis's character. I was at the reception desk at his residence in the Vatican *Casa Santa Marta* taking something out of my briefcase. As I lifted the briefcase, my red sash got snagged by the zipper. Next thing I felt tugging at my side. It was Pope Francis undoing the sash where it had become snared.

Francis himself tells sometimes, as a joke, that in the Vatican he is considered 'undisciplined,' in the sense that he does not wish to follow some of the pope's historic customs. At the same time, he is able to devote attention to everyone he meets, even simple and humble people. Where does this ability come from in your opinion? What does it reveal about the spirit of the Pope?

Pope Francis impresses me as someone, who, because he is not from Europe, does not feel restricted by European protocols which determine how a Pope should deport himself. In addition, because he was never based at the Vatican, he is not constrained by Vatican protocols which dictate how to be pope! Obviously, his life and ministry in Argentina has also formed his unique character.

In the last 50 or 60 years, the figure of the pope has changed enormously, especially in the way people imagine it. Also, Pope Francis is contributing a lot to this change. Some observers have spoken controver-

sially of 'desacralisation' of the figure of the Pope. How would you respond to this criticism?

The change in the image of the Pope began with Pope Paul VI, I would imagine as a result of the innovations introduced by Vatican Council II. The *'Tiara'* and the *'Sedia Gestatoria'* were duly abandoned. These were the beginning of a new style of papacy.

It was Pope St John Paul II who made the most radical changes to the lifestyle and ministry of the pope. The first and most noticeable were his frequent pastoral visits to different parts of the world. The most significant of Pope St John Paul II's innovations was the way he conducted the bishops' *ad limina* visits 'a visit every five years'. No other Pope had so many encounters with the visiting bishops.

At that time, the Pope and the bishop used to meet four times: in private audience, at morning Mass, at lunch, finally in a general audience with all the other members of the Bishops conference of that country.

Pope Benedict XVI retained the private and the general audience. Now Pope Francis does not have the private audience with each bishop. He meets the whole group together. One major feature of this group audience is the openness, frankness and informality. Another crucial feature of Pope Francis' encounters is that with him, there is no question that ought to be avoided. He desires open discussions.

Are the changes that Pope Francis has made irreversible? How far can they go forward?

The fact that Pope Francis changed his place of residence without causing a major cataclysm means that even the next pope could do the same. The more structured changes will be more difficult to reverse.

Pope Francis is a person who has developed a certain degree of 'celebrity status' with all the attention that he is attracting, also by people who are not Catholic and those who in the past may not have been interested in the Church. Based on his experience as a bishop, in contact with people, what would you say is the trait or traits of Francis that most impress people?

What one considers the most impressive trait that cause people to admire Pope Francis depends on where one is coming from in relation to him. For instance, many bishops would consider Pope Francis's words at the start of Synod 2014 to manifest his most significant trait. 'Speak honestly and openly, but listen humbly', he said.

Others, especially non-Catholics, warm to his simplicity and openness to all, but especially to those who might feel awkward around him. Most are deeply touched by his concern and outreach to the poor, the marginalised and the ignored!

Much has been said about his simplicity and sobriety. We think of the cars, such as the very basic Ford Focus model and choosing his residence at the guesthouse Santa Marta. Pope Francis does everything possible to avoid being identified as a powerful Pope-King of the past, surrounded by his courts. The world has met with favour the message he launched, but sometimes it seems to have brought confusion to the Church. Is that the case?

Many would regard Pope Francis's simple lifestyle and openness to ordinary people as far outweighing how they see him.

The simplicity and openness began to appear when he chose the name 'Francis' and did so 'in memory of St Francis of Assisi'. Second, he displays in almost everything he does the discipline and singularity of purpose which is often attributed to religious who regard the witness of their life and ministry as more important than any position or status they might have. The fact that Pope Francis carries his own briefcase attests to this simplicity of his self-image and self-esteem.

The press welcomed with much fanfare Pope Francis's many gestures and words, which seemed surprising and new. What is the occasion in which you personally were the most surprised by Pope Francis?

For those who observe Pope Francis closely, it has become second nature to witness yet another departure from the usual. Some of his surprising actions have been: taking lunch in the canteen with those who work at the Vatican; walking around Santa Marta doing his own chores; washing the feet of young offenders in a Roman prison, including two Muslims and two women among them; walking to the optometrist to get new specs!

Another aspect of Pope Francis which has warranted much attention has been his more or less strong and explicit complaints or criticism against the Roman Curia. Sometimes, it seemed that his opinion of the Roman Curia was not positive. Moreover, he was elected pope after a period marked by several scandals. What do you think of all this?

What was most surprising about Pope Francis's criticism of the Roman Curia was not the litany of faults which he listed, but rather that after listing all those faults and saying they needed to be addressed at once, he immediately went on to include himself. These are the principal faults upon which we must examine ourselves and repent for them!

The word mercy summarizes the meaning of Pope Francis's pontificate. In your opinion, why is Pope Francis so sensitive to this theme?

Right from the start, Pope Francis showed that his pontificate was going to be about 'looking out for' others. His gesture towards Cardinal Dias was a living out of what he had said when asked if he would accept being Pope, 'Even though I'm a sinner, I accept'.

For him what was most important was to admit the reality of his status before God and await the working of God's grace and mercy in him. It was only a short step to go from asking God's mercy for himself, to leading the Church to asking for it for all its members, indeed for mankind.

Pope Francis recalls often throughout his priesthood, he heard the confessions of penitents on various occasions and why this is necessary for him. Why is this experience so important for a priest?

Many people were extremely touched by the photo of Pope Francis presenting himself at a confessional in St. Peters to make his confession before proceeding to hear confessions. More recently there were equally touching photos of the Pope hearing the confessions of young people in St Peter's Square, during the Jubilee for Youth.

The highest point in the priest's ministry is, I believe, when he dispenses God's mercy, as he listens to a penitent confess his sins, counsels him and then absolves him from them and the eternal punishment due to them!

Often, Francis offers confessors much advice. Is there one piece of advice in particular that you try to put into practice?

The most touching and memorable advice offered by Pope Francis to confessors is, and I think will always be, 'I want to remind priests that the confessional must not be a torture chamber, but rather an encounter with the Lord's mercy.'

For the press, Pope Francis is a very popular character. In fact, much of the press internationally devote a great deal of attention to him. In your opinion, 'the Francis' that the press reports, is that the real Francis, the authentic one? Is there something that remains not said by media, therefore remaining in the shadows or not really seen or heard?

The media in general, but the press in particular, simply 'adore' Pope Francis, because he is a supreme source of eye-catching headlines! Second, they love his style of speaking and writing. He thinks, speaks and writes in soundbites. So, editors, 'Facebookers,' if you will, and Tweeters don't even have to rework his utterances, they simply transpose them.

The downside is that soundbites lead to laziness or economy of effort on the part of journalists. The Pope's quotes are so catchy that journalists and reporters tend to overlook both the context and the qualifications that are inevitable in any well-thought out papal utterance.

A prime example is the most infamous misquote: 'Who am I to judge?' The missing context was the question, which was aimed specifically at the 'gay lobby at the Vatican'. It was never about the Pope's opinion on gays as such. The missing qualification was the Pope's citing of the *Catechism of the Catholic Church*.

To quote his answer in full, 'If someone is gay and is searching for the Lord and has good will, then who am I to judge him?'

Sadly, once a misquote finds its way into the cyber-sphere, it never disappears and it is never corrected!

Some people say that Pope Francis is liked too much, by too many people. In this way, some try to suggest that he is not raising controversial issues, in order to avoid criticism. Perhaps even to the extent that they suggest he avoids that which could make some not like him. Have you ever happened to hear such a remark? What do you think about it?

Today, anyone who speaks the truth regardless of how self-evident, is bound to be verbally assaulted, especially in the social media. Pope Francis is no exception. Even his writings, which win acclaim from the majority of ordinary people, are heavily criticised by those whose 'sins' have been exposed. An example is *Laudato Si* which upset many by pointing out that their comfort zones of success, wealth and prosperity, have often been built on the exploitation of the poor and powerless.

Yet, Francis's teaching on the themes of the family, of marriage, and defence of life does not have the same impact. Why, in your opinion?

It is true. The media, especially the social media, have been extremely negative towards Pope Francis regarding his writings and speeches on marriage and the family. For instance, the substantial wealth of *Amoris Laetitia*'s teaching on marriage and the family is being lost, even neutralised by the overemphasis by the Pope's critics, because in their view he is 'overly-sympathetic' towards those who are in problematic situations such as civil remarriage after divorce.

In some instances, this is understandable, because much of *Amoris Laetitia* simply repeats and explains the Church's teaching on marriage, including the status of those in civil marriages after divorce.

Familiaris Consortio in particular is very specific about the inability of remarried divorcees to receive Communion. What causes real confusion are these soundbites by Pope Francis: 'The Church is a field hospital' and 'The Sacraments are not a prize for the perfect, but powerful medicine and nourishment for the weak.'

What is sad is to see people deliberately twisting or distorting the Pope's words of compassion and mercy so that they appear to be changing Doctrine.

After two Synods on the Family, what has changed in practice? Regarding *Amoris Laetitia*, there are many different interpretations. In your opinion, where is the novelty, if there is one?

I was not surprised by the reaction to *Amoris Laetitia*, and my lack of surprise was largely due to the highly publicised ideological positions taken up by the media, especially the Catholic media, before, during and after the Synods. All participants were conveniently put into opposing pigeon-holes or opposing camps, conservative or liberal, progressive or hardliner, and so on.

While the majority of those who have read *Amoris Laetitia* are positively impressed by it, there are those who want to tear it to shreds at every opportunity.

To tell the truth there are some positions that are extremely difficult for the African Church to understand or accept. Let me explain; two hundred years ago, European missionaries came to evangelise Africa's peoples. They convinced them that polygamy was wrong; that idol worship was wrong; that witchcraft was wrong. At the same time, they nurtured them to accept that Scripture, especially the Gospel, was the Word of God, which they would be living out by accepting and following the Church's teaching. That was the sure way to Salvation.

Accordingly, those who were converted had to take the most difficult step of abandoning their customs and traditions, accept the Christian Teaching and adopt its way of life and discipline instead.

Given the above, can the African Church retain its credibility if, after the Synods, it now goes to its members and says, 'We were wrong two hundred years ago, when we told you that you had to abandon all customs and ways of life in conflict with Christianity as it was presented to you then.'?

Are we supposed to say, 'In fact, today, it is quite in order to be living in an irregular marriage situation, as long as it is long-standing and there are children involved!'?

Or, 'You can receive Holy Communion even if you are living with someone to whom you are not lawfully married or if you have more than one wife, because you cannot turn the others away'?

Another issue on which Francis said strong words and made significant gestures is the theme of immigration in the world today. His repeated invitation is to build bridges, not walls. In your opinion, how far can you reach solidarity with migrants, without the reception becoming unmanageable for a given nation, or for society?

In a way the migrant crisis which is testing Europe and America's commitment to the principles of the *Charter of Human Rights* has long been a reality in Africa. As in North Africa and the Middle East, the trigger has been the actions of the West in the pursuit of material progress and prosperity. Africa has struggled for decades, during and after the colonial period, to find its own level after centuries of occupation.

From our experience, I would say there is only one workable solution, that being to stem the flow of refugees from the countries of origin. That is best done by concentrating on resolving the problems that create refugees and migrants. I believe recipient countries must invest more to bring peace and harmony at the source.

The theme of migration is linked to that of poverty. Francis always repeats that the essence of Christianity are the works of corporal mercy. He has made many significant gestures of solidarity by setting an example in the Vatican, in Rome and in his travels throughout Italy and around the world. Can it be said that, in this way, he has returned a bit of 'concreteness' to the Christian concept of human dignity?

What Pope Francis has done recently, namely bringing refugees back with him to Rome, in a way replicates what Churches in Africa have been doing already. To a large extent it is sharing the little you have, with those who have less or nothing. Most major dioceses in our conference area are doing more than their share in this regard.

Religions in this beginning of the third millennium have again become a very important factor in international politics, the cultural debate, and many social phenomena. Very often, religions have become causes of conflict and division between people and cultures. Is it possible to establish a dialogue between very different religions and cultures? Pope Francis, in this respect, expresses a very open, very confident approach. Is it a realistic attitude or not?

Had I not become actively involved in inter-religious dialogue and cooperation in the last eight years, I would not have been so confident as to say, 'One of the best ways to break the cycle of conflict between different religious communities is to establish and maintain an active inter-religious dialogue.'

What it does is to get us to sit down together and discover that despite our differences there are even more things that bring us together. Once the wall of strangeness has been taken down it becomes possible to recognise, accept and respect each other as fellow human beings with the same hopes and fears, dreams and expectations and above all the same need and desire to be loved and appreciated.

Pope Francis's journey in Africa was long, full of encounters and meaningful words. What did he leave the African Church?

For me, the main impact of Pope Francis' visit to Africa was threefold. At a time when many considered Africa a security risk, the Pope showed his commitment to share our fears and dangers. Second, his visit to Uganda highlighted that Africa has disciples of Jesus who will give up everything, even life itself, to show their love and fidelity to him. Thirdly, Pope Francis gave Africa the distinction of being the first Church to celebrate the extraordinary Jubilee Year of Mercy, when he officially opened the Jubilee with a wonderful celebration of hope in Bangui Cathedral. He did that at the very time that the Central African Republic was going through one of its worst political and economic crises.

The press and public opinion consider Pope Emeritus Ratzinger and Pope Bergoglio to be two very different personalities. In this undeniable diversity, in your opinion, is there something that unites them?

Yes, Pope Francis and the Pope Emeritus are very different. Nonetheless, there is a thread of continuity. Pope Francis made this clear on a number of occasions, beginning with his personal reception of Pope Emeritus Benedict into his new home when he returned from Castel Gandolfo, where he had gone immediately after resigning.

Second, they are both very strong on the New Evangelisation. One expresses it as 'Let nothing come between you and Christ your Lord!' The other says, 'Walk with Jesus; Build up the Church with your faith and works, and witness to Jesus by your life.'

Pope Francis has repeatedly said to regard his predecessor's resignation as an 'open door.' Can the papacy become an office or a fixed-term service?

No! Never! Already modern society is being torn asunder by a 'fixed term' culture, from marriage, to religious life, to the priesthood, there is a mentality that says, 'I won't do it for life but for as long as I am happy and fulfilled!'

Pope Francis is the first pope from the Americas in history. All statistical surveys say that Europe is no longer the centre of gravity of world Catholicism. Instead, the weight of African Catholicism is quickly growing. Can we say that the election of America's first pope in history could also open a door for Africa?

The experience of the last two Conclaves left me with the firm conviction that when the College of Cardinals gather to prepare for, celebrate and carry out the fruits of the conclave, the Holy Spirit is very much in evidence. When the Holy Spirit is present and active, the Church is capable of anything, including the election of an African who would be the best for the job at that particular time!

10 ADRIAN PALLAROLS

POPE'S SILVERSMITH AND DEAR FRIEND

A Parish Priest Became Pope and Remains a Parish Priest

The first time I met Pope Francis I said to him that I know you and he responded to me, radiant, and with a big smile, exclaiming, 'Son, brother, friend!' Why this enthusiasm from the Pope for your friendship?

WHAT CAN I say? I don't know! I suppose it is because he loves me like a son and really loves me! At times he says to me, that to him, I am like part of the family. I do not believe I can add anything else. He says, 'Son, brother, friend.' what else can one say about it? I can only add that his affection and friendship is unconditional. Unconditional!

In what other occasion did he call you, 'Son, brother, friend', in person or written?

When he was here in Buenos Aires, he used to give me books of art. Each time he would find such a book, he put it off to the side for me. When I went to him, often, before greeting each other, he would say to me, 'Wait a second. I have something for you!' Then, he used to gift me a book and I thanked him. One time he gave me a volume on the buildings that Bramante constructed in the Vatican. Now, it almost seems like a prophecy, as the Vatican would be his last home. It is in that book, he wrote the dedication calling me, 'Son, brother, friend'!

How did you meet and get to know one another?

The first encounter was in 2002 or 2003 during the restoration of the Cathedral of Buenos Aires. The office of the Archbishop was located very close to the Cathedral. Every so often, I would go there to see how the work was going and one day I met Archbishop Jorge Bergoglio who held my hand tight telling me that a person would explain to me what needed to be done. Then one day, he called me to create a medal of Mary, Untier of Knots, for which he has a great devotion. In 2005, we created a chalice together for his friend Pope Benedict XVI, and like this, in summary, is how we became friends!

I know that you have had a way to see how Jorge Bergoglio used to help the poor of the Archdiocese, also through your work! I heard that he used proceeds to help the poor, is that the case? How was this able to happen?

Yes, it is true. The Archbishop often used to bring me objects that he received as gifts and I used to sell them, delivering to him the proceeds. The Archbishop used to use that money for poor children, buying blankets, clothes, books, medicine and assuring this was all delivered to the poor.

There are many significant moments during your life in which Bergoglio was involved, your marriage, the baptism of your daughter Francesca and your son Mateo.

At a certain point of my life, I decided to abandon my family business. One day, the Archbishop received me in his office and I confessed this decision telling him, 'Father, today may I exchange some words with you because I am no longer working with the family? I do not have anything, only my shoes.' Just like that, after 25 years of working in the family business, an ugly situation had been created! The Archbishop said to me, the problem that regards you is my work, it is my mission, do not worry. I will take care of you. Remember here you have a friend. From that day I found again serenity and peace. I used to meet Fr Bergoglio every 15 days and when I did not go, he would call me saying, 'Where are you? What are you doing? Why didn't you come?' Finally, I opened my silversmith business and the day of its inauguration the Archbishop came to bless it spending a little time with us. Fr Bergoglio celebrated our wedding and the Baptism of my children. Often the Archbishop used to pass by the business because around the corner there is one of the most important churches of the city, The Most Holy Sacrament. When he celebrated Mass there, he would enter our work space greeting everyone, asking how we were and if everything was ok. Often, I would go visit him in his office to say hello and chat. He used to wake up very early, four o'clock in the morning, celebrate Mass, pray and then have breakfast.

Tell us something more about the time you passed together.

It makes me happy to remember when I asked him if he would perform our wedding ceremony and he said to me, 'Of course, my son, tell me the day and where I must go.' The story of my marriage is nice and I would like to tell it. The priest of my parish was very tough, severe, and cantankerous. The young ladies used to leave the marriage prep encounters almost in tears, because the priest used to scare them saying, 'If you do not do this or that I will cancel the date of the marriage!' During one of these encounters, the priest asked, 'Is there anyone here who will be married by a different priest? Raise your hand' We raised our hands and he asked who would be the priest. 'Fr Jorge,' I responded. He said,

'Make this Fr Jorge call me, he needs to ask my permission. If he does not do so, he will not be able to celebrate the Mass and I will cancel everything!' I responded, 'Do not worry. I will tell him.' In my heart thinking of that parish priest I thought to myself, 'You will learn a good lesson!' The day of the wedding while we were entering the church, the priest was there waiting for me, he took me off to the side and said, 'Why didn't you tell me anything? When your priest called me, I began to yell then I discovered I was talking to the Archbishop.' Laughing I responded, 'You said yourself to have him call you and that is what I did!' I think in that moment he would have liked to disappear in having raised his voice to the highest authority in The Church of Argentina. Probably from that day onward he did not yell at anyone else. We had fun with this, but for him it was terrible.

He felt humiliated?

I do not think that Fr Jorge harshly scolded or punished him, even if the priest raised his voice during the call. Fr Jorge only greeted him saying who he was and that he was calling for our wedding. The priest raised his voice and then asked the last name of Fr Jorge, discovering it was Bergoglio, Archbishop of Buenos Aires. Fr Jorge said, 'You shouldn't do this either with others, we are the same. Do not yell at me or anyone else! Be respectful to everyone', emphasizing, 'Be kind, this is work.' He advised the priest to be more available to those who wished to get married, because marriage is a special occasion to which God is witness.

What can you tell me about 'milk and cookies'?

At times, I used to without notice visit the Archbishop without having an audience. I used to say only, 'Father, are you busy, you have some commitment, some meeting?' He used to respond; 'No, I am free!' I used to ask, 'Oh great!

Can I stay with you a little and have a bit of coffee, milk and cookies?' 'Certainly', he would respond and prepared some for me and him. This tradition began thanks to two very elderly nuns that used to be with him and used to bake cookies when they were not praying. For Fr Jorge, it was normal to offer cookies. It is normal for a grandfather to offer his grandchildren cookies, to make them happy. Often, during these encounters we would talk about everything from history to art, various anecdotes, but often the conversation would focus on art because I teach this material at the university. He loves music and history.

Do you remember his favorite artists?

Michelangelo! Often, we spoke of how he constructed the dome of St. Peters, a great work of engineering. Fr Jorge used to like to talk about it because he has a mathematic-scientific formation, having studied chemistry. One used to share with the other what they thought about art, music, and we both used to stay distracted with this for 45 minutes, maximum an hour, before returning to work.

Is there a type of art or music that he likes the most?

Baroque artists, he used to tell me.

The press dedicates much attention to Francis. Do you think he enjoys this?

He was always a very, very reserved person and regarding this I will tell you an anecdote. Fr Jorge knew some secret passageways between the Archdiocese offices and the Cathedral. At times when we used to be together, he would say to me, 'Let's go this way, because outside there is the press.' It was interesting to pass through the tunnels constructed in about the year 700 and are still in good condition today.

Now that he is Pope? Do you think too much attention bothers him?

I do not believe so. Even if he has never loved the interviews, he respects the work of journalists. When he was Archbishop of Buenos Aires he would inform the journalists, with great notice, that there would be a press conference. He would respond to everyone, one by one.

Do you think he feels understood by the press?

Many times, he was judged by the press as a 'closed' person, simply because he does not love appearances. He wishes to speak with people without the press being present. Fr Jorge had the habit of going in very humble quarters, the worse places one could imagine, to speak to some 500 people at a time about their problems and worries. He never had the same interest for the big newspapers. As a journalist, you would have noticed that he prefers to give an interview to a small radio rather than a CNN. He is more attentive to the small than the big.

How did you learn of his election? What was your reaction?

I was working and I was not aware of anything! Everyone knowing that I was his friend was calling me on the phone saying, 'Turn on the TV! Watch what is happening!' This a bit saddened me: I thought it was a great thing for the Church and the world, but I lost a friend! I would never see him again like before. I went back home speechless! Thinking how far Rome is.

And instead?

The third day after the election the telephone rang, 'Ciao Adrian! It's Fr Jorge!' as if nothing happened [laughing]. He said to me, 'Do not be sorry. It is something I must do, that God wishes I do! Do not worry, I will never ever leave your hand! You will see that I will always be there with you, do not forget how much I care about you.' It was fantastic! In Buenos Aires he never used his last name but only 'Fr Jorge' and would say to me, 'Adrian! It's me.'

Were you left surprised by his election? What were other friends in Buenos Aires that knew him saying?

Many would not have ever expected to see him Pope. I had met him the day before he left for Rome. He always, at the end of our time together, accompanied me to the door of his office and asked me, 'Why do you have that face?' I responded, 'You know Father, I have the feeling you will not return.' He said, 'Do not worry for me. You know me! I do not like to travel and fly. I already have the ticket to return. When I return I will call you and we will see each other, ok? I will let you know, do not worry.' Instead it was the last time I saw him in Buenos Aires. It was I who was right!

What strikes you the most about his style and gestures as Pope?

I believe that many people are struck by his being a priest! He is a priest who truly acts and lives like a priest; but is also Pope, a priest turned Pope a simple priest. This is why he is so close to the people. This is the most revolutionary change, I see him doing.

What impact do you believe he is having?

I think that he is changing the Church as we have known it for the last 200 or 300 years. The way he approaches the people makes the people believe again in the Church. The people see him as a sensitive and humble man. Pope Francis lives like a poor person even if he is not and even if not living in a place of the poor. I saw his room and I could say there is absolutely nothing that could even distantly resemble luxury. It is an empty room, with a bed, a chair, a desk, and some sacred image of Jesus and of Mary on the walls. Nothing else!

He still calls you for your birthday?

Yes, always! It is one of the beautiful surprises I have the day of my birthday. He calls me always at different time, he never forgets. This is the most beautiful gift one could give me. It is a gift that touches my spirit.

You go to visit him often in Rome. How are these encounters? Do you find him different?

No, also with me, he is still the same person that does not use protocol. Obviously, I try to respect the protocol when there are other people present, for example a little while back, when there were the organizers and soccer players of Interreligious Match for Peace. However, if we are in private everything is always as it was in the past. When I talk to him on the phone and express my intention to visit him in Rome, he says to me, 'What are you doing? Why do you throw away money for an airline ticket? Stay there, do not waste money.' It makes me laugh a little [laughing].

Pope Francis entrusted you with creating the trophy for Interreligious Soccer Match for Peace (Rome, 1 September 2014), organized by the Scholas Occurrentes Foundation. You told me that during the audience with the soccer players the Pope asked for you. Could you tell me what happened?

Pope Francis changed the protocol asking at a certain point, 'And Adrian, where is he?' I remember then everyone sat down. There were many journalists from all over the world present. Pope Francis asked me to deliver the trophy to him in front of everyone, because he wished that everyone know who created the trophy for free. The Pope worries that my work is going well and that and my collaborators are fine. He says always that work gives dignity!

In your opinion, what does Pope Francis wish to bring to fruition?

It is only my opinion, but I believe that he would like to make the face of the Church more human. For the rest, it is that which he also tried doing in Argentina, going out in the street to seek, embrace, and carry the Church to the poor and needy. It is the change that he speaks about always; inviting priests, bishops, and lay people to go out to the needy taking care of them, helping them. It is an invitation directed towards the whole Church. He himself does not lose the occasion to stop and meet someone else; embracing children, the elderly, and the ill.

Do you remember in Buenos Aires when he used to take the bus?

Yes, of course, he used to do it often. One time, that I remember, I accompanied him to San Cayetano, a bit far from where I live about 45 minutes on the bus. Not able to travel back together Fr Jorge said, 'Do not worry Adrian. I have this.' He showed me a small slip of paper with the timetables of all the buses to take. He knew all the numbers of the buses, the hours and the travel times.

How do you think his being Argentinian influences his way of being Pope?

In all of his pontificate, there is something Argentinean. In Argentina there is nothing for certain, no one knows ever what could happen, that which will happen or what is about to happen. In South America it is all very unpredictable.

Therefore, at times you find yourself making unforeseeable decisions. I think that Pope Francis is a bit influenced by this unpredictability by being South American; he changes programs, makes unexpected trips and receives unscheduled visitors. Everything, obviously, happens for a good cause.

What does Argentina hope, having Francis as Pope?

Many Argentineans are proud of his election, because no one would have expected, in a million years, that this could happen—not only an Argentinean but a priest like him as Pope. His election, I believe, was not a low profile one. The seed was already planted at the Conference of Aparecida, Brazil, in 2007 when Cardinal Bergoglio indicated to the Church of Latin America the line to follow for the next fifty years. He wrote the final document and everyone said, 'This is the way necessary to follow.' It was then the world began dedicating more attention to Cardinal Bergoglio. When this thing happened, I realized that he began to go to Rome more often. I think, but it is absolutely my thought which Fr Jorge never spoke to me about, that Benedict XVI occasionally consulted him on certain questions, but this remains only my suspicion.

What does your daughter Francesca think about the Pope? She saw him recently as did your son Mateo, but he is still very little.

Francesca is nine years old, and in Buenos Aires she saw Fr Jorge very often. Since she is young, she does not have a precise idea of what it means to be Pope, especially because for her, it is so easy to meet him. She sends him often letters with designs and other gifts. She sees him like a sort of 'super friend,' recognizing how many people know him and love him. At times, she speaks about him, asking me if I sent him the designs and if I spoke with him. As if for anyone it was a simple thing. Francesca grew up knowing Fr Jorge as a dear friend that takes care of us. During my second to last visit to Rome, Francis sent a video message with him showing her designs and greeting her. She knows that the Pope cares a lot about her and how much we care about him. She also thinks that to speak with the Pope that all you have to do is dial the number, and it is because he wants it to be like that!

Can you tell us about the chalice with which Francis celebrated the Mass at Madison Square Garden in New York during his visit to the United States?

The Pope wants to make the poor understand, with symbolic gestures, how much he has them at heart. Therefore, I had an idea that I proposed to Pope Francis and he happily accepted. My idea was to create a chalice with which he would celebrate the Mass in New York during the September 2015 trip. Not just any chalice, but one made of many, many small pieces of silver, silver of small value like a little ring or chain, contributed by many simple and humble people. These simple pieces of silver would be fused together in such a way to create a precious object. The creation of the chalice was not made possible by rich and well-off people, but with the help of the poor, that donated a small silver object. This allowed many people who did not have the possibility to be near the Pope to be able to in that occasion feel themselves next to him. Pope Francis liked this chalice a lot, especially for what it meant, as if he could consecrate the bread and wine and drink the blood of Christ together with those not present. The day before the Mass he went to celebrate Vespers in St. Patrick's Cathedral. Inside the church, there were few people, because the space was limited, but outside there were so many who could see him for so little time. That chalice allowed so many people in the Eucharistic Celebration to be there with him, in his heart.

Is there still something else you would like to say regarding Pope Francis?

At times, people ask, 'Is the Pope really like what you see on TV?' I respond, 'He is man and priest as always, as he has been the past 55 or so years.' Before, few noticed him, because few knew him. Now being the same person, everyone knows him. Now he can help and announce the Gospel as Pope to many more needy people in every part of the world.

11 Cardinal George Pell

Prefect of the Secretariat for the Economy

The Most Important Thing in the Life of the Church is not Money

I would like to ask you first of all about when was your first encounter with Jorge Bergoglio? Did you know him before he was elected Pope?

I DO NOT PRECISELY remember the first encounter. We were both members of the Congregation for Divine Worship and the Discipline of the Sacraments and also of the post-Synod Council. I did not know him well, but I remember before the last Conclave we spoke together a bit.

During that time, did you observe something in particular?

No, we spoke about the life of the Church in general.

From your first encounter with Pope Francis, could you tell us something that surprised you? I imagine there was something that left an impression.

For the outside world, it was all a surprise. Many times, in the newspapers one reads inaccurate versions of the truth and this is particularly true of a Conclave, especially because those who know don't speak, and those who don't know speak. It was a historic moment in the Church because it was over 1000 years since a Pope was elected from outside of Europe. I personally was not surprised when Francis was elected.

You come from a very far place, Australia, and Francis is the first Pope to come from the Americas. Is coming from a very far place, with respect to Rome, a help for the Universal Church?

One time I asked Francis, 'Holy Father, is it you who comes from the ends of the earth or me?' and he responded, 'Both of us, even if from diverse extremes!'

It is our being here in Rome, both he and I, that is simply a sign of the universality of the Church. We come from two different worlds, he from the Hispanic Latin American one, I from the Anglophone one. This is good for the health of the Church, to have this variety of origins of culture. Catholic simply means universal.

Pope Francis undoubtedly receives much attention from mass media. In your opinion, is there something about his teachings that is misunderstood?

Yes, especially in newspapers that are expressions of the lay world, I have often encountered points of view on the left, even some censorship. If, for example, Francis speaks of the devil, speaks of the impossibility of ordaining women, against abortion, sometimes all of this is simply not reported. The consequence is that the Holy Father is seen especially by those that are outside the life of the Church from too narrow a perspective.

From the beginning of Pope Francis' pontificate many speak about 'reform' of the Church. You are also a member of the so called 'C9,' the Council of Cardinals tasked with studying a draft of reform of the Roman Curia, as well as Cardinal Prefect of the Secretariat for the Economy. Therefore, you play a role at the forefront in the construction of these reforms. In your

opinion why did the moment arrive at the present time for the Church to face these reforms?

There are two types, at least two sides to the reform. Obviously, I have more to do with the economic, financial reforms, but there is also the reform of the Roman Curia and changes in the life of the Church in a vaster sense. We in the Council of Cardinals, the so-called 'C9', are not a group of revolutionaries. We are a group of cordial friends, in all sincerity. There is a climate of cordiality among us. There are points of view in some ways different from each other, but we are there representing different continents to represent effectively the diversity of the Church. Already there were changes in the structure of the Pontifical Councils announced as well as major changes in other dicasteries. Concerning the economic and financial aspects, the changes are even greater and more important, but here there is a reason, the request came universally from the cardinals. In response to the scandals in the past of the so-called IOR, the Institute for the Works of Religion, and also inside the Vatican, we have achieved substantial progress that would have been impossible if it were not for the support from the Holy Father. Already it seems to me one could speak of irreversible reforms. However, there is still more to do and we have great plans. We only have to implement them.

You speak of irreversible reforms. Do you believe that with reforms Pope Francis is bringing to fruition, it will be possible to proceed without turning back?

I cannot make prophecies for the future. There are certain things that are unchangeable due to their nature, for example, the already defined doctrine, sacraments, papacy, and so on. The political future of the popes is all another argument. Anyway, I already said publicly that I believe with the financial reforms a point of no return has already passed. There are achievements like transparency and personal responsibility ('accountability') that will necessarily be conserved because the financial reforms had already been agreed to by the entire spectrum of cardinals as well as by wider Catholic opinion.

Moreover, I hope that innovations like the Council of Cardinals will not be cancelled, because to me it seems very useful for the Pope to have the ongoing ability to meet several times a year a group of advisors and discuss many matters over the course of two or three days.

Let us stay on the subject of this very articulated reform Francis has put in motion in the managing of economic affairs. I am sure you have spoken about it quite a few times. In substance, what does Francis desire from these reforms?

I for the greater part of the year visit the Pope every two weeks to discuss the economic reforms. What would he like? Simply that we administer the patrimony with effective criteria and justice. He is aware of the importance of implementing universally adopted procedures in this area: for example, the role of the Auditor General is very important, and the office dedicated to money laundering, AIF (Authority of Financial Information.) These are fundamental institutions, thanks to which, many things have changed. Also, another thing he always desires is that everything that is done benefits the poor.

Is there a resistance against the reform Pope Francis wants?

No. There could be a tiny amount of resistance, but the people who worked in this realm in the Vatican are largely in agreement for adopting these reforms, because in the end there is nothing particularly unique. They are universal standards, modern procedures that need to be adopted, but ultimately no great innovation. Furthermore, this is an interesting point, the financial reform is something that unites all the cardinals also outside the Roman Curia. All cardinals that are oriented to the left or right want this reform, want the goods that the Church receives and possesses to be used well without negligence or waste, and with honesty.

To change structures, institutions, modify a name or role of some office, seems relatively easy. Yet, I ask you, is it enough? What is truly needed for reform?

All the movements in the reform in the Church, in general, in 2000 years of history, were essentially a return to the sources—Jesus, the Gospel, the Apostolic tradition, everything that began with the teaching of Jesus. I think now of a particular quality of Francis that strikes the people, the simplicity of his style of life, poverty, truly that which Jesus spoke about, poverty and poverty in the spirit.

What is it like to work with Francis?

It is interesting because the Holy Father has quite a personality and is a man of faith and prayer. Yet he still has the capacity and courage to speak in a very direct way, and sometimes in an unexpected manner. Therefore, it is interesting to work with him.

When you say unexpected, can you give us an example?

Yes, this is a good question. Francis has written and referred many times to a 'progress in building a people in peace, justice and fraternity', that in his opinion, as he explains in his Apostolic Exhortation *Evangelii Gaudium*, 221, 'depends on four principles related to constant tensions present in every social reality.' One of these is 'time is greater than space,' a reason for which the Pope advocates 'creating processes,' rather than 'occupying spaces of power.' For someone Anglophone, this formulation is very unusual and interesting.

Economy and finance are very serious matters, but also Pope Francis is said to have a great sense of humour. Has it ever happened that you both have exchanged some joke or something humorous even when speaking about economic questions?

In a way, yes, the Pope has a good sense of humour. Something that strikes me is that one can say anything, anything you want to say, without him demonstrating any sign of disapproval. You can say the truth as you see it. Then obviously he responds. Yes, he has a good sense of humour which he does not lose, even if every so often he could seem tired since he is working very hard with all his responsibilities, at his age, as the Successor of Peter.

A reoccurring theme in the teachings of Francis is the condemnation of the idolatry of 'dio denaro' (the god of money). When money is adored as an idol, human dignity is sometimes trampled. Is today's economic system truly this ruthless?

Obviously, Pope Francis' view of money comes basically from the Gospel, the Teachings of Jesus. Jesus spoke very harshly against greed, being well aware that money can 'imprison' people and can capture people's hearts. Then, beyond this, he was Archbishop in Latin America, in Argentina, and we all know well in those countries there is great inequality between the rich and the poor. He has matured this sensibility towards the poor and the suffering.

In general, he speaks about the economy, work, distribution of wealth, safeguarding of the environment, in very strong, direct terms, with accents that perhaps we were not used to hearing, to this degree, in Church teaching or preaching. Sometimes he has even been accused of being a 'communist' or 'anti-capitalist' Pope. What do you think of these accusations?

First of all, it is wrong to argue a lack of continuity between Francis and predecessors, back to Leo XIII. There is a line, a social doctrine of the Church already very well developed, very sophisticated, always evolving, but it is already something marvellous.

Certainly, the Holy Father is neither a communist nor socialist in any way. In Argentina, he was attacked because he was not following the way of Liberation Theology. His line, I do not remember precisely the name, above all put the accent on faith and the religiosity of the people. The Pope is simply against injustice, as all Christians need to be. Regarding the concept of 'market', definitely the Pope contests its excesses. Even today, we see, it is an imperfect institution, but nevertheless it has created much well-being. It is enough to think of today's Europe and its average standard of living.

Pope Francis and his gestures, also those related to wealth, money, and consumer goods, are often presented as revolutionary. Are we really in front of a revolution, or with Francis, is there continuity?

It is not a revolution. The Holy Father understands the importance of public gestures, and through them, wishes above all to demonstrate that riches are not a sign of God's blessings. This he continually teaches us in not only words, but especially with gestures. For example, in the past, the choice to go around in a bus instead of taking a Mercedes or the fact that he does not go on vacations outside of Rome and I think that he does this, even if he does not explicitly say it, because the poor do not have the possibility of going on vacation and he therefore remains at his home too. I remember when he was just elected. He went to pay the bill for where he was staying, a sign that he was like all the others. These gestures are not revolutionary in a political sense. They are spectacular, important symbolic gestures in the tradition of St. Francis of Assisi.

In the last few years, much was done in the Vatican for setting out a new course in the managing of economic affairs, like the Vatican Bank and others. Do you feel confident in affirming that the scandals belong to the past?

It is difficult to say it with absolute certainty, but certainly, the IOR President, Jean-Baptiste De Franssu, has done very well. They closed 4,000 accounts. The AIF, Financial Information Authority, in charge of counteracting money laundering, is an office that functions very efficiently and correctly. The IOR does not launder money. We hope, and I believe that I can assure you, that in the Vatican, there is no longer the corruption that existed in the past. The imperfections that exist are, for the most part, remnants of the past. Anyway, we will work until they will no longer exist.

The famous American Archbishop Paul Marcinkus, the president of the IOR, in the 70s through late 80s, was reputed to have said that the Church cannot go ahead only with Hail Marys. Is there any truth in this affirmation?

Yes and no. Certainly, the Church cannot go ahead without prayer or without faith. Wealth becomes a danger if the Church becomes too rich, if it begins to believe that with such wealth the faith is not so much important. Man 'does not live by bread alone' (Mt 4:4), but neither are we Manichaeans! Money is not a demon! Having said this, Catholics and all the world have the right to demand that the Vatican administers income, property, and investments with honesty and confidence, so that the works of the Church enable faith and charity to go forward.

Francis has said, 'St Peter didn't have a bank' an affirmation that was welcomed with much favour by many people. How should we interpret it?

The Pope in this way simply affirms that the most important thing in the life of the Church is not money and this is absolutely true. One time, speaking at the annual Meeting of Rimini, organized by the Communion and Liberation movement, I publicly affirmed that it is easier to organize finances than to bring about a conversion. After that, all the secular press, reversed the words reporting that I said it was easier to bring about a conversion than to organize the finances. This demonstrates the materialistic mentality of the world of communications.

The Vatican City State is an independent and sovereign state and for a state like that of the Vatican it is very useful to have its own bank even if its existence is not completely necessary.

There has been much talk about strong resistance, more or less hidden, to the changes in the managing of Vatican finances. Do you sense there is resistance to your actions, to your works?

When one changes something, there is always some resistance. Many do not want changes, they do not like them. Perhaps some fear losing something. There is always the possibility that a small group does not want to be brought to the light, because then they would see their mistakes or something perhaps worse. I would not speak of great opposition. If anything, there may be a small group who oppose the reform, but the great majority of those that work in the Vatican are not involved with them.

Pope Francis expressed right away his desire to have a 'Church which is poor and for the poor.' Is the Church adapting to this desire and what is needed to be done in this regard?

I say that in the Church, everyone needs to live being poor in spirit, according to the Teachings of Jesus and the Gospel. In the Church, everyone is called to perfection, but not everyone to the radical material poverty in which for example St Francis of Assisi lived. As I already said, when the Church becomes too rich there is always the danger of losing the faith, prayer, the transcendent dimension.

The First Commandment says to love God, the Second, your neighbour, and so on. I often remember a citation from Margaret Thatcher, who, as a politician, was of course a great champion of the free market. It is a very appropriate phrase in our context, is very well-known and in substance says that were the Good Samaritan not to have had capital and some wealth, he could not have paid for the help that he offered to the person who had suffered robbery. The same could be said for the Church!

At times, the press pits Francis and Benedict against one another, are they that different from one another or is there continuity between them?

The personalities are a bit different, but I would say continuity. Yes.

Is there a last consideration you would like to add regarding Pope Francis?

First of all, I think it is important to emphasize what an enormous force for good Pope Francis has proved to be. He brings sincerity and passion to his role as pastor of the universal flock and people respond to that. He has great communication skills and has been able to reach people and raise the profile and the positive image of the Church as a whole. All of this is a very great achievement.

Through him the papacy has a unique presence in the world at large and it is important to preserve that unique opportunity.

Maybe it is important to reiterate that the Pope is only one person! One Successor of Peter and if he resigns, he is no longer the Successor of Peter. Maybe in the future it would be helpful to clarify that should a Pope resign (even though I know that on this point there is discussion) he remains a Bishop and might be reappointed as a Cardinal and might be known as pope emeritus. However, in my opinion he should not wear the white papal soutane and convention should dictate that he does not write or speak on Catholic doctrine or life, especially on controversial areas.

The unity of the Church is important and it is not a given. It is sufficient to notice that at the Pan-Orthodox council in Crete in June 2016 some attended but others didn't. Unity is a miracle and we need to be careful when we speak, in my opinion in a mistaken way, of two Popes and also of how we speak about synodality. Obviously, we do not want an exaggerated centralism that has been so clear in the history of the Church or the teachings of Francis, but no one wishes a Church divided into national blocks or continents.

Unity and diversity is not always an easy balance to achieve, but it is very necessary and Pope Francis is providing valuable leadership as we find our way forward in this challenge.

12 RABBI ABRAHAM SKORKA

CHIEF RABBI OF BUENOS AIRES & DEAR FRIEND OF POPE FRANCIS

Love the Lord Your God and Love your Neighbour as Yourself

by Michael Hesemann

M Y NEXT DESTINATION was Belgrano, an elegant quarter in the north of Buenos Aires. Luxurious houses and expensive cars revealed the upper middle class of the capital city. Many Germans settled in this region, and until the 1950s there were even bi-lingual schools here. Many Jews came as well in the first wave of refugees which reached Argentina in the 1930s. Rabbi Fritz Leopold Steinthal, who had fled in 1938 from Münster, Germany, founded a synagogue one year after his arrival in Buenos Aires. This synagogue was named after his teacher, the great German Rabbi Leo Baeck (1873–1956). In its Torah ark (*Oraun Ha-kaudesch*), Torah scrolls saved from the burning Synagogues in Germany found a new home. The new house of God soon became the center of German-Jewish life of the city, and two daily newspapers in the German language were printed until the years after the war. It would be here that a very different chapter would be written with regards to the relation between Catholics and Jews which had complications that the founder could not even imagine.

The name of the man with whom I had an appointment in the Belgrano Benei-Tikva-Synagogue was Dr Abraham Skorka. He was not very tall, his thick, short grey hair was combed back and made way for a wrinkly high forehead.

Two warm brown eyes sparkled with intelligence from behind his horn-glasses, while his lips were formed into a mischievous smile. He seemed more a philosopher or scientist than a Jewish man of God; but yet, he might as well be the most significant Rabbi of our time. Extraordinary not only because he was a doctor of chemistry and had worked as bio-physicist in research before he received his vocation, something not all too different from the career of the pope; but extraordinary first of all because he took literally the importance of Jewish-Christian dialogue, most of the time very literally. He became the best personal friend of the then Archbishop of Buenos Aires, who was to become a cardinal and later Pope, Jorge Mario Bergoglio. I wanted, I had to, meet this man and I was overwhelmed by the friendliness with which he received me, a German Catholic.

My Argentinian colleague Mary Molly Hamilton-Baille had accompanied me as an interpreter. We soon realized that our conversation could take place without any major obstacles. Rabbi Skorka speaks fluent English, but also German with a cosy Jewish accent. His parents, who fled from Poland to Argentina, had taught him this language. He asked us to take a seat in his small office as to tell us the story of his most uncommon friendship with Jorge Bergoglio.

Rabbi Skorka gave me the following account.

Everything began in the end of the 1990s. I was, as every year, invited by the President of the Republic to take part in the celebratory Te Deum *as the Jewish representative. This is a prayer commemoration which is celebrated every year on the day of our independence, 25 May, in the Cathedral. It takes place in the company of representatives of all religions present in Argentina and all denominations. As you might know, football is also very popular with us, and so a simple way of entering into contact with a person* is by asking him for which team he roots. Before the Te Deum, priests visited us and greeted us and wished us a good Independence Day. Archbishop Bergoglio came and asked for which team I was rooting. I answered that I was a fan of River Plate, which is the home team of Belgrano. I asked the Archbishop, 'And you'? 'Of course, San Lorenzo', he laughed, since San Lorenzo had been founded by a priest. Good, it was understandable why he was a fan of that team; a true fan, as I would discover later.

One year later, 25 May 1999 to be exact, after the Te Deum, one of the Secretaries of State dealing with religious affairs approached us and explained that the President was expecting us. We were supposed to get in line to greet the Archbishop and the Apostolic Nuncio and subsequently be led to the President. Since the President was very busy, the secretary was very insistent that we only greet the President briefly with a handshake, not make long speeches, and a wish for a good Independence Day. Bergoglio and I have one thing in common, both of us do not like protocol. We do not like to be rushed. If the President wanted to see us, then he would have to be a little patient! So, I wished the Archbishop well, congratulated him on his homily and spoke a couple of words with him, just to break protocol. Only 20 seconds, I thought, that is nothing! 'Your citation of Jeremiah was well chosen', I told him, and that was all. He looked very deeply into my eyes.

Let me also briefly explain that the fans of the River-Plate received the nickname 'the chickens' since they had to wait 24 years to win the championship. It is said that they are helpless like chickens, which is obviously hurtful. Bergoglio looked deep into my eyes and said as only response to my comment on the verse of Jeremiah, 'This year we will eat chicken soup!' In that year River played just really badly and San Lorenzo played really well. I *paused and did not know at first what to think of this answer. A fraction of a second later, I could not hold back and said, 'Oh that is really mean!'*

The Apostolic Nuncio looked at us helplessly and whispered in a severe tone, 'You cannot say something like that in Church!' Bergoglio calmly explained, 'We are speaking about football.' 'Ah!' the Nuncio responded, 'well then go on'.

As bitter as it sounded, I understood that behind this joke lay a deeper intention, a very different message. There was a man, who wanted to signal something to me, that being, 'If you want to speak to me, you know that I am a very normal human being as you are.' Forget the protocol. There is no wall between us. The doors are wide open. That was the beginning of our friendship. We exchanged letters, congratulations on our respective feasts, and I asked him questions. We met again in the other Te Deums and at prayers for peace. In 2004, I invited him to Slichot, the prayers for forgiveness before the Jewish New Year. I asked him for a greeting to our community. He came twice, that year and in 2007. Every time, he gave fantastic speeches. The second time, he stayed until the midnight prayer. When I took him home, he repeated, 'Believe me, in all honesty, I have felt the prayer! I really prayed with you.' That was a very beautiful experience for me.

The period of our really intense collaboration were the years, 2010, 2011 and 2012. We met in this time at least once a month.

In 2010, we wrote a book together, On Heaven and Earth, *which became a bestseller worldwide. It was the only time in history that an archbishop and a rabbi published a book together. It deals with all the questions which the simple man on the street asks to our religions: How does one prepare for death? How can we deal with the problems of our time? What is money? Is it an idol? Are we not worshipping idols today? What can we say about the basis of our religious traditions and our worldviews, which have so many common values and roots?*

We ultimately venerate the same prophets! In the beginning Christianity was a movement within Judaism. In the Acts of the Apostles, everyone can read how the apostles disputed with Rabbis about the Gospel.

I had to interrupt him, and argued that until the Council of Jerusalem in the year 48, one had to be a Jew before receiving Baptism and being received in the first community of Christians.

That's exactly what Bergoglio said, too. After our book had been such a success, we met during 2011 and 2012 regularly to appear together in a TV-show for the channel of the Archdiocese in Buenos Aires. We spoke about the same subjects, namely friendship, family, what it means to be happy, and many other themes which might interest the simple man on the street.

Then I asked the Rabbi whose idea it was to write the book.

That is a good question. I had the idea to write a book about theological and philosophical questions. One day I asked my friend, Jorge Bergoglio, 'Could you please write one chapter about God?' I wanted to ask other great philosophers and thinkers for their contributions and compile a nice anthology with all the material. He was reluctant at first and explained that he was not internally ready to write a chapter. A couple of weeks later he called me, 'Let us write a book. A book about God, the devil, evil, friendship, the conflict of Israel and Palestine, and politics. Not from a theoretical philosophical perspective and not in the highest intellectual and linguistic fashion, but for the simple man.' This is typical for Bergoglio: he speaks and writes very profound things, but in a very simple language.

Of course, he was right. This was the book which touched the people!

And I can reveal something else about our friendship. As Sergio Rubin, his biographer, worked on the book El Jesuita, *he asked Bergoglio whom he would suggest as an author for a preface. He immediately answered: Rabbi Skorka! I felt that as a great honour to write the preface of a book on a Cardinal, now Pope, as a Rabbi. I asked him, why did you suggest me to do that? He answered without hesitation, 'It just came from the heart.'*

I can tell you another story. When we had conversations for the book, I always went to his place. He lived right by the Plaza de Mayo in the general vicariate. Then all of the sudden he said, 'I cannot expect from you to drive through half of the city to come to me. Next time we will meet at your place.' I did not want that at first, he is 14 years older than me and his health is not at its best, but he insisted. We had a table set up in the entrance of the synagogue at which we both sat and had our discussions. He always came Tuesday morning. We put croissants on the table and discussed about God and the world.

Then he shocked me. On 11 October 2012 the Pontifical University of Buenos Aires had an hour of celebration marking 50 years since the opening of the Second Vatican Council. There he endowed me with an honorary doctorate. I could not even believe it. It was the first time that a Pontifical University granted a doctorate to a Jew and a Rabbi. He was the chancellor of the university. When we looked at each other, as he gave me the document and the cameras flashed, he whispered to me, 'You cannot imagine how long I have waited for this moment.'

When I saw him after his election to the papacy on the balcony in his white cassock, it was to me as if between this image and my eyes, the eyes of my friend appeared. I thought to myself, well, a new era has begun. Our transmissions, our books are now history. Literally history, a new thing begins now!

It might sound strange, but when I heard that Benedict XVI resigned, I told my wife: just wait, but my friend Jorge Mario will become the new Pope! Why? I do not know why. I have no rational logical explanation for it. It was just a hunch. I felt that Bergoglio was a man who was needed by all mankind in this time, not just by the Catholic Church. He is a man that respects all faiths, is deeply rooted in spirituality and justice, and who respects every man. He acts with the same spirit as the prophets which are at heart the common heritage of the Jews and the Christians.

Without respect for one another, we cannot create a reality in which God reveals himself to man. To approach God means in the first place to approach a neighbour with respect. To honour God means to love one's neighbour. 'You shall honour your God' and 'love your neighbour as yourself' are the Commandments of the New Testament as well. Bergoglio embodies exactly that. Bergoglio knows, that theology without peace, love, justice, and charity is only intellectual mock fencing. Theology must be a reality, something expressed in everyday actions. We both believe, Jews and Christians, where there is hatred, God cannot be. That is a Mitzvah, a law of God, you shall not hate your brother!

In order to establish peace, you have to build up a serious, honest relationship, and that we can do with Bergoglio. He is not bound by political norms. He knows how to behave correctly in a political way, but he does not act politically correct. As I have known him, I am sure, that he will do everything to bring about a major U-turn, not just in the Church but in the whole world! He wants to condemn injustice and poverty and everything that degrades man. That is the Bergoglio that I know. With the help of God, he will change something in each one of us despite the fact that the changes will be uncomfortable for some people. He knows that he serves God. God does not tolerate injustice!

Bergoglio is very compassionate towards every form of human suffering. When someone approaches him, and tells him that he is homosexual for example, he would not reproach him. He would try to understand him with great patience and tell him to see that our morality cannot accept this, but that he sees in him a brother. He wants to help him deal with his problem. However, for Bergoglio, when it comes to robbery, murder or exploitation, he has no tolerance.

How serious he is about that is revealed in the afore-mentioned book, *On Heaven and Earth*. There, Bergoglio is cited saying why even today, as Pope, he does not give Holy Communion to select chosen individuals during Papal masses, as his predecessors have done; and also, why he holds back very visibly during papal audiences:

> It's true that among the parishioners there are people, who have killed not only according to the spirit or physically, but also indirectly by bad use of capital or by payment of unjust wages. Maybe they belong to philanthropist groups, but do not pay their employees what they owe, or make them work under the table. This is the hypocrisy, the schizophrenia I spoke of before. Some of those we know the whole curriculum of, we know that they call themselves Catholic, but they have dirty behaviours and repent nothing. That is the reason why, in some occasions, I do not give Communion: I remain in the background and let other helpers give Communion, because I do not want these people to get close to take a picture with me ...

What will Bergoglio as Pope change in the Church? How will the Church look in the future? I was curious what the Rabbi would say about his friend in this regard.

[Abraham Skorka answered after a pause of thought.] *I think he will change the core. I do not know if he will change something liturgically. I do not think that he will revoke celibacy, in all these questions, he is very conservative. His revolution is of a spiritual nature. In all scandals which were brought up in the media, such as the Vatican bank, homosexual priests, he has no tolerance. He will fight to bring about a Church of humility, a Church for the poor, those financially and spiritually poor. He will establish a Church of purity. Other things are less important to him. What is relevant for him is the purity and integrity of the Church.*

Once he has accomplished that, then he could take a next step. Before one starts to make a religious change, one has to be pure. Otherwise, it is impossible. If that is not the case, it is just like changing a decoration. We have spoken much about scandals and I believe I know his viewpoints pretty well. His problem now will be, how can I show Catholics and the world another Catholic Church? In this light, you have to look at all his actions. Concerning that, which is our main theme, is the question, 'How can we make another step, a second step, in the dialogue with the Jews?' This is a subject which is very close to his heart.

13 CARDINAL PETER KODWO APPIAH TURKSON

PRESIDENT OF THE DICASTERY FOR PROMOTING INTEGRAL HUMAN DEVELOPMENT

Simplicity is an Evangelical Witness

I would first like to ask you if you knew Jorge Bergoglio before his election as Pope.

I MUST ADMIT THAT even if we were together at the Conclave that elected Pope Benedict XVI, we did not really know each other much. Once, I met him in Argentina, at the Sanctuary of Luhan, when I was returning from a conference that took place in Rosario. I met Cardinal Bergoglio at the Sanctuary, greeted him and engaged in a small talk. This was my first meeting and knowledge of him before the last Conclave.

After the election, was there an encounter that left a particular impression?

Working for him, and with him, it is difficult to talk about a specific encounter, since each meeting has its own purpose and meaning. Going back instead to the Conclave, the incident that struck me, and I suppose, everyone else, was the choice of the name Francis. This, as I discovered later, was Cardinal Bergoglio's way of expressing his sense of the Church's need to pay particular attention to the presence and the needs of the poor. This would become the heart of the message of his Pontificate. Concern for the poor, those on the periphery, the excluded would become a *leitmotif*, we could say, of the pontificate.

**Pope Francis surprised everyone when he decided to
make his first trip outside Rome to Lampedusa, to
express solidarity with the migrants. He would then
do the same gesture in Lesbos. Never before has a Pope
given so much attention, in person, to such tragedies.
Are these acts reflecting the times of today?**

That gesture in particular struck everyone. Casting our
minds back to past popes, we notice, for example, what
Archbishop Roncalli did in Turkey during the Second
World War for Jews; but he was not yet a Pope. The visit
to Lampedusa struck everyone, that is true; but I also think
of his first Holy Thursday visit to a juvenile detention
centre. For Lampedusa, in particular, one could ask
oneself, 'Why does the Pope go to meet migrants, and not
to some sanctuary or cathedral to celebrate a Mass?' As I
have observed before, such care for the poor and broken
lives, whether they be people or creation itself, is the
leitmotif of Cardinal Bergoglio's ministry, as a Pope; and
it explains his taking the name Francis.

Cardinal Bergoglio is a pastor in the true sense that Jesus
used and applied the expression to himself. The pastor
turns back to search for the lost sheep. The migrants who
cross the Mediterranean are, we could say, like 'the lost
sheep' from their land of origin, from their families, from
their culture. The attention, the care for the poor and the
fragile is the true hermeneutical key of this pontificate.

**The voice of Francis is considered more influential than
the voice of any political leader. It is a worldwide
spiritual authority, also beyond the borders of Catholicism. In your opinion, what is the basis for this authority?**

It is an authority made of authenticity by simplicity. If I
may use a popular American expression, he is an example
of 'one who walks the walk and talks the talk.' Above all,

he is credible. The genuineness of his gestures lends him credibility and authenticity, and confer on him moral authority. It's a bit like in the Gospel, where 'people were astonished at the teaching of Jesus, because He taught them as one having authority and not as the scribes' (Mk 1:22). Indeed, the scribes used to quote and appeal to an authority outside themselves.

The source of authority of Jesus is His person, Himself. With great humility, because of the incomparability of the two subjects, one might consider Pope Francis as inspired in this regard by the life of Christ.

You also make a comparison between political leaders and religious leaders. This is not an easy comparison to make. The task of politics, according to the Church's Social Doctrine, is to take care of the ordering of society for the common good of its citizens, advisably, through the exercise of political charity. In this sense, a religious leader can have no objection to cooperating with political authority. In fact, this calls for cooperation. In this sense, the moral authority of a religious leader, like Pope Francis, should be an asset and an inspiration to political leadership. This, I think, is what Francis seeks to do.

Is it this authority that also strikes the politicians who meet him?

When he was elected and shortly after his inaugural Mass, the Vatican Radio organized a series of interviews with the cardinals present in Rome. Many of them spoke about Francis's simplicity that speaks for itself, his credibility, as well as the spirit of Franciscan poverty in all he does. I could not help but concur with these sentiments expressed by cardinals and non-ecclesiastical figures, including political figures who, apparently, knew him better than me in those early days.

Subsequently, if the political leaders come to visit the Holy Father, I would imagine that it is not only out of curiosity. Knowing that true leadership is not exercised with power, but with trust and being considered worthy of trust, I would not find it strange that leaders visited and continue to visit because of trust in his leadership and personal virtues. The Letter to the Hebrews says this, speaking of Moses and Jesus who were considered faithful in the Household of God, Moses as a servant, and Jesus as Son.

I suppose that when Heads of State meet the Pope, they find that he is worthy of trust because he lives for the Church and for the wellbeing of the human family. His Encyclical Letter, *Laudato Sì* is a proof of this, just as his visit, for example in the Central African Republic. Driving through clouds of dust to smile and greet a sorely tried people, made one of them observe, 'The Pope loves us. He loves us and he takes on great risks in order to be in our midst.' For the people, the Pope is worthy of trust and attracts people to him. The people know they can trust in him, his leadership, judgements, and teachings. The political leaders feel the same as the people.

The Church has a great patrimony of Doctrine on social themes like the distribution of wealth, the fight against poverty, the defence of human dignity. Now, with Pope Francis, we could say that there are themes that really come to the forefront thanks to some expressions he has emphasized like the 'globalization of indifference', 'the throwaway culture', slave labour, and so on. This effectiveness of the teaching of Pope Francis has to do with language, emphasis, or is there something greater?

Something more, certainly! What could it be? These teachings of the Social Doctrine of the Church are like the essence of the Gospel in the Bible, the sources of faith. There is not a Christian that does not believe God created humanity as a family, establishing brotherhood as the principle of living together; where brotherhood means that we derive from the same womb, brothers share a common dignity.

Then, if we are all brothers, every act that brings the elimination of another man is a fratricide! On the opposite side there is solidarity, the caring for and committing to the wellbeing of one another. Using the resources of the planet at our disposal is an example. We have the principle of the universal destination of the goods of the earth. These must be available to all and shared equitably.

When Francis tackles the themes you mentioned, his inspiration is simply the biblical faith, according to which indifference wounds the sentiment of our common humanity. So, if brotherhood is the basic principle of human coexistence, how is it possible to become indifferent to one another, toward our brothers and sisters? Indifference is almost the antechamber, if you will, of fratricide!

The Pope has reserved many cordial encounters and appreciative words toward people and groups often 'far' from the Church. I think of the encounter with popular movements in Rome and Bolivia, for example. What type of 'strategy' is this?

This strategy corresponds to the sense of brotherhood that we spoke of earlier. If you are convinced that the basic principle of the human family is brotherhood, then every man and woman matters, as a brother and a sister, even if we do not share the same faith. If these people and groups are far from the Church, this is not significant. What did Jesus say? He came for the distant, the lost, the sick. These were far from established worship and religion at that time. They existed on the peripheries of social and religious structures of their days; and Pope Francis speaks of a Church going out, as a missionary Church, to the peripheries. If the Pope goes toward the people and groups you were referring to, he does so simply in the name of the brotherhood and of a humanity redeemed in Jesus, the firstborn of many brothers!

The Pope has received much criticism as a 'Third Worldist', 'anti-capitalist', or 'populist', in the popular sense. Do you think there is truth to these accusations?

In my opinion, these are exaggerated and misleading criticisms. I know people who consider them downright bigotry. 'Third Worldist.' Why? Because he brings attention to the Third World? Then tell me, why did Pope Paul VI write an Encyclical Letter on *"The Development of Peoples" (Populorum Progressio)* in a period of the emergence of several colonial countries into independent states?

On the basis of what do we judge him? For the travels in the Philippines, for example? Or patronising the organization of Meetings of Popular Movements? Or the creation of Cardinals from counties, hitherto unknown to people in Europe? This is not being a 'Third Worldist'. This is a Church that is universal and must live its nature and manifest her characteristics, going out toward the peripheries, and making everybody *count* in the household of God. We are all members of the Catholic Church, even if one comes from a dusty Central African Republic or from a little known Fiji Church. Why should one not welcome and recognize those Catholics who live there?

When the Pope went to Sweden 31 October 2016 for the joint commemoration of the 500-year anniversary of the Protestant Reformation with the Lutherans, this was a gesture of attention toward the periphery, toward such a small Catholic minority. We do not say 'Third World', because this expression usually connotes poverty and underdevelopment, and Sweden, instead, is rich. Therefore, more than being a 'Third Worldist' I would say that the Pope is only carrying out the mission of the Church toward the peripheries, the fallen away, the neglects and tiny fragile Churches.

Additionally, you also ask for my opinion about the criticism of the Pope as an 'anti-capitalist'. Many times, I have had to answer this question with regard to the encyclical *Laudato Si'*, especially in from many countries in the Western world.

The Pope is not against capitalism. Maybe he is more favourable to a system like the one in force in Germany or Holland, a 'social market economy': namely, a 'social' economy, capable of responding to the laws of the market. An economy that knows how to respect the person. Francis desires that the economy serves man and not the reverse. He is not a socialist or communist or anything like that.

When Pope Leo XIII wrote about the right of people to own and have capital, it was that, in freedom, they would respond freely to a sense of responsibility towards others in society. Likewise, when in *Centesimus Annus* Pope John Paul II extended the sense of capital to talents and endowments people may have, he quickly referred to their responsible use for others in society. How different is this from Pope Francis's call for attention to the needy and neglected in our midst? The free exercise of responsibility towards society is missing!

In a way, Pope Francis, simply recalls what is written in the Bible about everything created needing to serve the needs of the human person, and business helping to make this possible by processing raw material of nature into specific needs of humanity.

Even if Pope Francis is more favourable to a social market economy, it does not mean that he is anti-capitalist. He is against the abuses of the market, against an economy that kills, because *oikos nomos*, the administration of the resources of a household to serve the needs of the household is failing in its task. This is for various reasons, including the removal of 'finance' from serving a true economy, making finance a business in itself outside of the economy yielding to all forms of speculation. It can generate monies which then do not serve true economy and are stashed away in tax havens and offshore accounts, that generate a dead economy which spreads its odour of death! Making any human activity aware of its responsibility to society and the dignity of its members is the beginning of a call for ethical thinking and conduct.

Turning then to 'populist', I'd say right away that I do not think the Pope fits that description. He does not chase popularity, nor is he a rabble-rousing ideologue about a social condition. The attraction of people toward him is not something he seeks. He wishes only to encounter people where they are at, and in compassion, and not from a balcony, to listen with the heart and touch their situations.

Francis is the first Pope to dedicate an entire encyclical to the theme of the environment. In your opinion, what inspired Francis? Is it a personal sensibility or perhaps, today, in the world are environmental problems getting much worse?

Let's start from the first Mass, celebrated at St Peter's on the Feast of St Joseph. There Pope Francis reflected on the image of St. Joseph, as custodian of the Holy Family. The reflection of the Pope extended this image of being custodian to all present at the Mass. He invited us all to be custodians, in particular, of the family and then of the poor, namely, the two types of fragility in our midst, the poor and creation. This was at the first homily.

One could go back to the Encyclical Letter of Pope Leo XIII, *Rerum novarum* (1891). While that Encyclical focussed on the conditions and rights of workers, it also contained some seeds of current ideas about our natural environment. For example, it stated that those who receive God's bounty in the form of natural resources or property should exercise their responsibility 'as the steward of God's providence, for the benefit of others'[1]

But it was Vatican Council II that inspired a committed study of the relationship between man and his environment. Having formulated for herself the mission of showing solidarity and respectful affection for the various experiences and problems of man as he or she journeys through history, the Church of the Vatican Council II and post-Vatican II displayed a sharp and a keen interest in the role and the place of the environment and nature in man's response to and pursuit of his vocation to develop. especially, in the Apostolic Constitution, *Gaudium et spes* (1965). Blessed Paul VI then, in his Encyclical Letter, *Populorum Progressio*, made this striking statement, 'By dint of intelligent thought and hard work, man gradually uncovers the hidden laws of nature and learns to make better use of natural resources. As he takes control over his way of life, he is stimulated to undertake new investigations and fresh discoveries, to take prudent risks and launch new ventures, to act responsibly and give of himself unselfishly.'[2] In *Octogesima Adveniens* (May 1971), Pope Paul VI further addressed the inseparable relationship, interdependence between human life and natural environment, saying: 'Man is suddenly becoming aware that by an ill-considered

---

[1]   Encyclical *Rerum novarum*, Leo III (15 May 1891), 22.
[2]   *Populorum progressio*, 25.

exploitation of nature he risks destroying it and becoming in his turn the victim of this degradation. Not only is the material environment becoming a permanent menace—pollution and refuse, new illness and absolute destructive capacity—but the human framework is no longer under man's control, thus creating an environment for tomorrow which may well be intolerable.' (§21)

Already in his first Encyclical Letter on the human person *Redemptor Hominis*, Pope St John Paul II warned about the threat of pollution to nature.[3] In *Sollicitudo rei socialis*, Pope St John Paul II, called for respect for nature, and for the first time, also respect for the nature of the human person. There are, then, two environments to respect: that of nature and that of the human person. Later in *Centesimus annus*, he drew attention to what he termed the ecological question and its connection with the problem of consumerism. Here he referred to a widespread anthropocentric error, namely, our failure to recognize that our capacity to transform and in a certain sense re-create the world through human work is always based on God's prior and original gift of all that exists. Man might imagine that he can make arbitrary use of the earth and subject it without restraint to his will. Rather than carry out his role as a co-operator with God in the work of creation, man sets himself up in place of God. The final outcome is a rebellion on the part of nature which is more tyrannized than properly governed by him.[4]

Pope Benedict XVI developed the Church's teaching on ecology and the environment further, describing in his Encyclical Letter, *Caritas in veritate*, not only an ecology of nature, but also 'an ecology of the human person', and 'a social ecology' and 'an ecology of peace'.[5] 'Social ecology'

---

3   *Redemptor hominis*, 11.

4   Encyclical *Centesimus annus*, John Paul II (1 May 1991), 37.

meant two things importantly, that protecting the environment means improving people's lives, and that environmental degradation and underdevelopment are closely interdependent.

With all these teachings, the background was prepared for Pope Francis to teach 'an integral ecology' and call urgently for listening to the cry of the poor, because they are our brothers and sisters. And, the cry of the earth because it is our mother, our lives are drawn from it and our lives depend on it.

So, it is both personal sensibility for the two fragilities, the poor and creation, and an urgent need for change in lifestyle and attitude towards creation and its gifts to humanity. The need to recognize the interrelatedness and the interdependence of all things is foremost in the thinking of Pope Francis, and *Laudato Sì* is for that matter a social encyclical. It is not just about ecology. It is about the life of the human person, and how the ruin of one is also the ruin of the other.

Francis is the first pope coming from the vast areas of the so-called developing countries. What does it mean or signify? In your opinion, in which aspect of Pope Francis's pontificate is his coming from this part of the world most evident?

Cardinal Bergoglio has relatives in Italy! His family emigrated to Argentina, didn't they? Certainly, Argentina is south, for its geography, but not the south that implies underdevelopment. Anyway, he comes from a part of the world where Church life is different than the European experience. Pastoral life is a bit different than in Europe. There they may dance samba. In Europe, you may do waltz.

---

[5]   *Benedict XVI Message for the celebration of the World Day of Peace* (1 January 2007), 8.

While in Europe theologians fight over the reformability of dogma, there they discuss 'liberation theology', and so on. Maintaining the same faith, which makes the Church Catholic, his world has sought to give expression to and to live the articles of faith differently in a different culture.

So, his election to be Universal Pastor of the Church is a call to enrich the universal Church with all his experiences. I will give some examples. If in Argentina he took care of ill priests, he has brought this experience with him. If in Buenos Aires he used to travel on the bus, also this experience he has brought with him. His simplicity is not something he decided upon in Rome, he brought it from there. And even his way of being a pastor for the Church! It is up to us to open up to and be enriched with the wealth of diversity of a Church that is universal!

If tomorrow a new pope will arrive from Asia or Africa, he will enrich the Church in the same way!

Pope Francis speaks concretely of works of corporal mercy, of touching the flesh of the poor, and he himself has offered the poor many concrete gestures. Can we say that he has brought back a bit of concreteness to the concept of human dignity?

Yes, certainly we can affirm that his gestures have really demonstrated how much concreteness there is to pastoral care of people with dignity. This dignity involves above all respect, then awareness that the dignity belongs to all of us, and it is not taken away or diminished by illness or some other negative experience in life. It is a base quality of each man. My mind goes to the Pope hugging the sick, especially the sick, whose condition makes hugging come with difficulty, like lepers. In this way, yes, Francis demonstrates a truly concrete respect for human dignity. I am in agreement with you.

One speaks often about the simplicity, sobriety. We think of the cars, the choice of residence. Pope Francis does everything possible to avoid to be identified as a powerful Pope-King of the past, surrounded by his courts. The message that he has launched here has met much favour, but sometimes it seems also to have brought a bit of disarray in the Church. Is this the case?

I do not know if it is! Yes, the car is small and simple far simpler than my car that was a gift. Yes, he lives in Santa Marta House, and not in the papal palaces and so on.

You ask me if I see a bit of disarray in the Church. Certainly, even the radicalism of Jesus brought disarray among his disciples. The Gospel entails some challenges to accept and recognise. Pope Francis also challenges us. Just a few days ago, a Cardinal was telling me that leaving his apartment he was approached by two journalists who were asking why cardinals live in such large buildings, whereas the Pope lives with simplicity. He did not respond, despite the journalists insisting, because the press in those days were focusing on cardinals living in luxury. Let's not confuse space size with luxury. The apartments in San Callisto are large, but nothing that you can call luxurious.

When Pope Francis was once asked about living in Santa Marta, instead of the Papal palace, his answer was that he prefers to live together among people and not isolated. He added then that if someone does not agree with his choice to live in Santa Marta, it's fine. Surely no one can take away his freedom to live where he wants to.

However, here in this room where we are now, as in the dicastery offices and in my apartment above, there is no luxury. Certainly, the rooms are big, because they are old buildings. One day an architect friend visited my apartment and on entering the living room exclaimed, 'here there is space for four rooms'! I do not see luxury, at least not in my apartment. When I arrived here in Rome, I went to Ikea to buy some of my furniture!

The Pope, like any bishop, tries to respond to the demands of the Gospel, where we all read Jesus' saying: 'Foxes have dens and birds of the sky have nests, but the Son of Man has nowhere to rest his head' (Lk 9:58). This is the simplicity of life that we are called to embrace.

The first words of Francis were welcomed with almost overwhelming enthusiasm, namely, 'How I would like a poor Church for the poor!' Are these words relevant today? Is the Church in tune with Francis on this point that is so sensitive for public opinion?

In a certain sense, numerous images of Jesus in the Gospel truly invite us to be poor for the poor. Let's remember for instance when He speaks of the rich, the camel and the eye of the needle. Indeed, this is a metaphor; but if one does not unload a camel, it cannot pass through certain alleys. Jesus took this example to show that we cannot get to certain places with excess baggage, and too much of it! We need to shed some baggage! Make ourselves trim for the sake of the Kingdom. If we live with simplicity and poverty, we can get to places!

Many times, we are overloaded with truly unnecessary things.

When Francis speaks of wanting a poor Church for the poor, it is because when one is poor one knows how to entrust oneself to the grace of the Lord. In one's poverty, one discovers that the source of all that is worth our struggles and anxieties, all that is necessary in life is the Lord. When the temptation to consider other sources of security takes over, there we are already in danger.

The poor Church is a Church which is more faithful to its real origin, nature and to her Founder. We are all poor before the Lord; and the Jubilee Year of Mercy has helped us discover this. We are poor because we need the grace of the Lord!

14 HIS BEATITUDE FOUAD TWAL

PATRIARCH EMERITUS OF JERUSALEM FOR LATINS

An Energetic Advocate of Respect for the Human Person from Conception to Natural Death

When was your first meeting with Pope Francis, or if before the election, with Cardinal Bergoglio?

ON 15 APRIL 2013, Pope Francis received me and a delegation of bishops and priests from the Diocese of Jerusalem. I presented a paper in preparation for the Pope's next meeting with former Israeli President Shimon Peres, dealing with some matters that he should speak about with the President. My presentation had five points. At the third point, the Pope stopped me and expressed his desire to visit the Holy Land. I told him his desire was the fifth point on my list!

Is there a certain encounter with Pope Francis or Bergoglio that has left a special impression?

Yes, the special impression occurred during his visit to Bethlehem, while he had dinner with six poor Christian families. I remember that he could not eat, as he was so deeply involved in listening to their plight. One of the papal entourage, at a certain point, told the Pope that he had 20 minutes to rest before his next engagement; to which the Pope replied, 'I cannot leave, look at these suffering families.'

A second impression happened when the Pope, upon seeing the Separation Wall, remained silent and then tapped the shoulder of the 'popemobile' driver to stop. He got out, went to the wall and prayed silently for a few minutes. I recall sharing, at the time, with some in our company that this gesture will spread around the world in five minutes. Long after the Pope's speeches are forgotten, that gesture would be remembered.

From your point of view, when looking at the teachings and pastoral style of Pope Francis, what has impressed you the most?

After his election, when Pope Francis stepped onto the balcony at St Peter's Basilica it was clear he had a different style of papacy in his mind. He spoke simply. He chose the name Francis rather than choosing a name from the long list of his predecessors. This choice signalled a new emphasis on poverty and simplicity.

His simple style and down-to-earth preaching calling listeners to a personal relationship with Jesus, with an emphasis on God's love and mercy explained why so many are attracted to him.

Almost every public message from Pope Francis has included the word 'mercy'. Those who define a revolutionary pontificate as liberalizing the Church's teaching on issues such as marriage will likely be disappointed in Francis. By constantly emphasizing mercy, he has made clear that he expects the Church to apply its teaching with compassion. The potential downside is that, without calling for repentance, the fruit of which is mercy, a false understanding of mercy could spread.

It was clear from many leaked documents that emerged in the months before Pope Benedict's resignation that the Vatican was in crisis surrounded by allegations of financial mismanagement, corruption and infighting; and this, at a time when the Church's reputation was already in tatters after decades of cover-ups of child sexual abuse.

Pope Francis attempted a shake-up of the hierarchy, appointing an eight-man cabinet of cardinals from outside the Vatican. Though some changes are being implemented, nevertheless the results are not as evident as his initial enthusiasm.

Undoubtedly, Pope Francis with his teachings and his witness has brought the world's attention to the major global issues of globalization and its imbalances, such as the gap between the rich and poor, hunger, exploitation of nature, and so on. Why, on these points, are his teachings so effective and attract so much attention?

The Pope boldly says the rich who exploit the poor are bloodsuckers. This bold statement surely has attracted attention. While acknowledging that riches in themselves are good, they are relative, not absolute goods. He criticized the so-called 'prosperity gospel', a religious belief among some Christians that financial blessing and physical well-being is always the will of God for them, and that faith, positive speech, and donations will increase one's material wealth.

He has also spoken of the exploitation of the people as a form of slavery. The serious matter of human trafficking, he soundly condemns. These and many of his words attract attention.

Take, for example, the issue of poverty. Pope Francis has repeatedly said that the essence of Christianity is living out the corporal and spiritual works of mercy. Then, he himself, in practice, has made gestures of solidarity. Can it be said that Pope Francis has, in this way, returned a bit of 'concreteness' to the concept of human dignity?

Yes, I believe he has heightened people's awareness of human dignity. For example, when the world's leaders seek strategies for solutions to social problems in combating poverty, he demands that the dignity of the marginalized must be respected. He is a strong advocate of respect for the human person from conception to natural death.

Religions in the beginning of the third millennium have again become a very important factor in international politics, in the cultural debate, and in many social phenomena. Very often, religions are factors of conflict, divisions between peoples, between cultures. In this context, what does the voice of Pope Francis represent?

As Pope, when he is dealing with terrorism, he cannot come forth with details. He must speak but remain non-partisan. Pope Francis's talent for personal communication, from his accessible speeches to his Twitter remarks and heartfelt personal phone calls, has not gone unnoticed. His abilities as a communicator do not stop with young, disenchanted Catholics, promoting transparency and approachability within the Catholic Church, and making himself known as a public personality. He has made apparent his potential as a diplomatic person and his interest in mediating international conflicts and relations.

When he speaks, people listen. He has the moral authority to speak to all nations.

Nowadays how can one establish a dialogue between different religions and cultures? What has your experience in the Holy Land taught you?

In Jordan, 'dialogue' between different religious is relatively easy. Dialogue is done with friendship, because of our tribal system. Our social relations there are very good.

In Israel and Palestine, dialogue between different religions and cultures tends to be political. As you know, politics is based on interest, self-interest more so than the interest of what is right. The dominant side bulldozes its way until it gets what it wants. Just look at the huge number of victims from Middle East politics.

Pope Francis, on the theme of interreligious dialogue, shows a very open, trusting attitude. Is this a realistic attitude, or a bit naive?

Only time will tell if this openness is naïve. Recall when Pope St John Paul II vehemently opposed the war in Iraq, many thought he was naïve. When Pope Francis underlines the importance of friendship and respect between men and women of different religious traditions, the noisy voice of the world charges him with naiveté. Christians in Europe are being challenged to be more open to different cultures, religions and traditions. The most recent terror and violence by radical Islam stymies genuine interreligious dialogue. He can remain open, but he must always be prudent in statements about Islam.

Can a true interreligious dialogue be established with Islam, without neglecting the theme of human rights?

Charity is the language that everyone understands. The basis for interfaith dialogue should be the acknowledgement of every human being's humanity and basic dignity, regardless of their religious or any other background. If we wait for Islam to respect human rights we will have a long wait. The fact that human rights are not respected in Islam is all the more reason for engaging in dialogue with it. If we never have dealings with Islam, then there is little hope that of itself, it will come to understand, respect and implement human rights.

These first years of Pope Francis's pontificate coincided with the establishment of ISIS in Iraq and Syria, and with terrible and bloody attacks in Europe by terrorists who reference Islam. Francis said on the return flight from Krakow in July of 2017, that the 'war' we are fighting 'is not a religious war', and that he does not like to talk about 'Islamic violence.' Some judge this response as too soft or too prudent, what do you say?

As I said earlier, the Head of the Catholic Church cannot speak in details about Islam, that is for the scholars and other commentators. At the same time, it was very disappointing to hear of him speaking to journalists aboard his return flight from Krakow. Pope Francis said that violence exists in all religions, including Catholicism, and it cannot be pinned to one single religion. To suggest that there is 'Catholic violence' is wrong. There is no evidence of violent Catholic fundamentalists at work anywhere in the world. That the head of the Catholic Church would suggest such is simply remarkable. The Catholic faith does not in any way advocate the use of violence. Islam has many verses that do.

Let's take the specific issue of human dignity. This concept has a very strong value in Christianity, evidenced more so than by many other religions. We think about the question of freedom of conscience, of personal rights. How do you then enter into dialogue with other religions in order to protect or safeguard Christian teachings on human dignity?

We enter dialogue to educate and enhance others' understanding of human dignity. Such dignity originates from God and is of God because we are made in God's own image and likeness (Gn 1:26–27). Human life is sacred because the human person is the most central and clearest reflection of God among us. Human beings have transcendent worth and value that comes from God; this dignity is not based on any human quality, legal mandate, or individual merit or accomplishment. Human dignity is inalienable. This is the Christian message and this understanding should be common to all who believe in God.

What was the legacy of Pope Francis's visit to the Holy Land?

I think he came to the Holy Land with great optimism more than realism. He wanted many good things to happen. For many people, his simplicity and gestures were greatly appreciated. Some were very disappointed, especially in the Arab culture, upon witnessing the Pope kissing the hands of several Jews. In Arab culture, to kiss the hand is a gesture indicating courtesy, politeness, respect, admiration or even devotion by one person toward another.

The good idea of the Vatican Garden meeting with President Mahmoud Abbas of the State of Palestine and Israeli President Shimon Peres did not produce tangible results. Israeli Prime Minister Benjamin Netanyahu responded almost immediately with front-page news of further apartment expansion in East Jerusalem.

The tree, planted during the ceremony in the Vatican Gardens, still grows without interference from media noise. One hopes that his ideas will grow because the work of grace is inside the heart and humans cannot measure its growth, only God.

In the Middle East, in general, and also in the Holy Land, the number of Christians is dwindling. What consequence can this diminished presence of Christians in the Holy Land have for the universal Church?

Many Christians from the global North and West still have a hard time seeing and relating to Christianity in the Arab world as living, vibrant communities of faith with rich spiritual and theological traditions. This may be partly due to a lack of understanding about the shape of Christianity in other parts of the world. Christianity in the Arab world has had a long and lively history, including in Palestine, where one still finds today communities of faith that stretch back thousands of years to the very beginnings of the Church, where Arabic is spoken in liturgies and sermons. The Church has played an integral role in the development of society, whether in terms of providing leadership in very difficult times or in pioneering valuable social services like education. War and persecution has led to a haemorrhaging of Christians from the Middle East, particularly from Syria and Iraq. Christians are an essential part of Middle Eastern history and culture, and they continue to contribute powerfully to society, particularly in the fields of education, medicine, science and engineering.

Christians add a diversity of perspectives to public discourse and thus help encourage critical thinking in society. Without Christians, there would be little space in Iraq for intellectual curiosity and critique.

Sometimes, the West's attitude, in general, and also, some say, the Church, seem too timid in light of the persecution of Christians on the part of Islamic fundamentalism. Why, in your opinion, is there, as some say, timidity?

Many Western Christians have, for the most part, lost confidence in their own Gospel and Christian culture. Christianity built cathedrals, built universities, built hospitals, allowed commerce to flourish, abolished slavery, fostered science, laid the foundation of democracy, treated women as equals and converted empires. When this Christian culture is acknowledged, it can meet the challenge of Islam. Sadly, it has been eroded in most western countries. I think one of the factors behind the timidity that goes with this, is that in the face of Islam, we have few leaders of countries willing to openly defend the Cross of Jesus Christ.

Muslims coming into western countries do not share the liberal values embraced by western culture, namely, homosexuality, same-sex marriage, and so on. They have their religious faith and culture, whereas, most western nations have abandoned the Christian faith and are completely secular. There is no zeal or passion, therefore, to defend persecuted Christians.

The Catholic Church has been working on interreligious dialogue for some decades already, after the Second Vatican Council. According to you, what novelty will the pontificate of Pope Francis produce or what steps forward will it bring?

It is difficult to say what steps forward, if any. Matters of doctrine are very complex and the dialogue already in place will continue. I think Pope Francis's openness and also that of the Ecumenical Patriarch Bartholomew of Constantinople will encourage greater openness for a dialogue of friendship. We always had this openness and friendship in Jordan prior to the Second Vatican Council. Vatican II, for the first time since the split of the Christian churches, gave an authoritative word on ecumenical dialogue in its Decree on Ecumenism.

Printed in July 2021
by Rotomail Italia S.p.A., Vignate (MI) - Italy